Barbara Duff is an expert in psychosexual and relationship counselling. An accredited member of the National Association for Professional Counselling and Psychotherapy, her work and writings are also informed by her thirty years as an educator.

Barbara is author of *Rekindle the Spark – 10 Steps to Revitalise Your Relationship*, published by Orpen Press and *The Ten Secrets to a Happy and Long Lasting Relationship*, available on Amazon. Barbara's innovative online self-help programme for couples *Rekindle the Spark – Save Your Marriage* is recognised and endorsed by counsellors worldwide.

This book is dedicated to all those couples who have taught me so much about connection and commitment, resilience and respect in their efforts to enrich their marriage.

And to my precious husband, Desmond, who continues to teach me the true meaning of love.

Barbara Duff

HAPPILY EVER AFTER

A guide for engaged couples

AUSTIN MACAULEY PUBLISHERS™
LONDON • CAMBRIDGE • NEW YORK • SHARJAH

Copyright © Barbara Duff (2021)

The right of Barbara Duff to be identified as author of this work has been asserted by the author in accordance with section 77 and 78 of the Copyright, Designs and Patents Act 1988.

All rights reserved. No part of this publication may be reproduced, stored in a retrieval system, or transmitted in any form or by any means, electronic, mechanical, photocopying, recording, or otherwise, without the prior permission of the publishers.

Any person who commits any unauthorised act in relation to this publication may be liable to criminal prosecution and civil claims for damages.

A CIP catalogue record for this title is available from the British Library.

ISBN 9781398401976 (Paperback)
ISBN 9781398401983 (ePub e-book)

www.austinmacauley.com

First Published (2021)
Austin Macauley Publishers Ltd
25 Canada Square
Canary Wharf
London
E14 5LQ

Table of Contents

Foreword	9
Introduction	10
Chapter 1: Why Get Married?	13
Chapter 2: Who Am I?	22
Chapter 3: Who Are You? Knowing Your Partner	31
Chapter 4: Building a Healthy Relationship	39
Chapter 5: Communication	48
Chapter 6: All About Feelings	61
Chapter 7: Dealing with Conflict	69
Chapter 8: Revealing the Hidden You	79
Chapter 9: Let's Talk About Sex	84
Chapter 10: Being Part of a Team Without Losing Your Identity	96
Afterword	129
Bibliography	130

Disclaimer

The author and publisher of this book have used their best efforts in preparing this guide.

The author and publisher make no representation or warranties with respect to the accuracy, applicability, fitness or completeness of this guide. They disclaim any warranties implied or expressed, or liability for any loss or damage, including but not limited to special, incidental, consequential or other damages.

If required, the advice of another qualified professional, who is familiar with the particular circumstances, should be sought.

The author and publisher do not warrant the performance, effectiveness or applicability of any websites listed in this book. All sites are for information purposes only and not warranted for content, accuracy or any other implied or express purpose.

This guide contains material that is protected under international copyright laws and treaties. Any unauthorised reprint or use is strictly prohibited.

Foreword

So, you and your partner have decided to get married? Congratulations! This book is dedicated to you. Committing to getting married is no doubt one of the most important steps you have taken in your lives so far. I hope that you feel supported by your family and friends, and that you are happy with your decision. Here, you will find a pre-marriage programme designed to help you and your fiancé(e) explore and deepen your relationship. In *Happily Ever After*, you will learn skills and techniques to help ensure that your marriage is a happy and fulfilling adventure – the gateway to a wonderful future.

I wish you both every happiness in your life together.
May there always be sunshine.

LOVE AND MARRIAGE

A thought transfixed me: for the first time in my life I saw the truth, as it is set into song by so many poets, proclaimed as the final wisdom by so many thinkers: the truth that love is the ultimate and highest goal to which man and woman can aspire.

Viktor Frankl
Man's Search for Meaning

Introduction
Working with Happily Ever After

Remember those fairy tales from your childhood? The handsome prince, the beautiful princess, and lots of obstacles in between. But no matter how many challenges they had to cope with, love and fate conquered all. And the story usually ended with a blissful wedding and the great line:

...and they all lived happily ever after.

Fairy tales and romantic novels have a habit of ending just as the happy couple set out on their life journey together. We rarely get to see how and if they succeed in having a happy married life.

Here in *Happily Ever After* you get a glimpse into some of the challenges and joys that can face couples once they have committed to being together for the rest of their lives.

Making Time for Just the Two of You

There is so much excitement when an engagement is announced. Friends, family, everyone wants to share in the buzz. The questions are unending – when are you going to get married, have you chosen the venue, not to mention the menu? What about the dress, the honeymoon, the wedding guests – and don't forget that Auntie May has to be invited no matter what.

But while this excitement is fun or sometimes overwhelming, it can mean that the two people at the centre of it all are forgotten. Once the whirlwind starts, you and your fiancé(e) need to make sure that you make time to be together, just the two of you. Time to relax and time to laugh; time to talk and time to think; time to plan and time to share.

Happily Ever After takes you through the most important aspects of a loving relationship. I have chosen these topics based on nearly thirty years of working with couples as a relationship and psychosexual counsellor.

Each chapter addresses one key topic. Contained within each chapter you will find either a Quiz or Reflection exercise. The quizzes are designed to help you identify any potential stress points in your relationship. The exercises will teach you the skills you need to address these issues in a non-confrontational way.

Once you and your partner have mastered these techniques, you will feel better able to face the future together, confident that you can deal with whatever challenges it may bring.

Try reading this book together. It's best to do the written exercises separately, and then share your thoughts and feelings with your partner.

Take it slowly – maybe just a chapter each week. This way you get to focus on one aspect of your relationship at a time. Some of the topics covered here may have been no-go areas for you and your fiancé(e) until now. If that is the case, by talking to one another and doing the exercises, you will realise that nothing awful will happen when you address these topics. In fact, the more comfortable you feel to discuss personal or intimate issues with your partner, the more meaningful your relationship will become.

The Troubleshooting Guide at the back of the book gives further insights and practical suggestions to help address any issues that may arise for you. This way you can nurture, protect and deepen your relationship, ensuring a lifetime of mutual love and happiness.

May your wedding day be as wonderful as you have dreamt. It marks the start of your marriage – a journey that will hopefully be lifelong, joyful, and fulfilling. Your careful preparation means that you will both enter marriage with the confidence and the skills to deal with any challenges or difficulties as they arise.

Chapter 1
Why Get Married?

The married state can be defined as a socially sanctioned sexual relationship involving two people whose union is expected to endure. Sociologists Horton and Hunt define marriage as the approved social pattern whereby two people establish a family. The family is one of the lynchpins of society. It is in this basic social unit that most people, as children, have their first experience of love and attachment.

The Merriam-Webster dictionary defines **engaged** as being absorbed, attracted, pulled, captivated, pledged, involved, as well as pledged to be married. When we are emotionally engaged, we give very special attention to the loved one. We gaze at them for longer, touch them more frequently. This is known as being emotionally present to one another.

The motivation to get married is multi-faceted but usually includes the desire to introduce stability and a sense of permanence to a relationship, as well as the desire to establish a home and start a family. Deciding to get married is a testament by the couple of their conviction that this relationship can be for life. The search for a life partner is over. From now on, they want to share their lives with one another.

The ceremony of marriage involves a public declaration by the couple of love, honour, and mutual respect. Wherever a couple choose to make their marriage vows – in a vaulted cathedral, a country church, a temple, mosque, or registry office, it is the couple themselves who are the celebrants. They take centre stage and accept the responsibility of honouring their commitments. The promises made on the wedding day include that of remaining faithful to one another through hard times, as well as happy, in sickness and in health. Such a deep commitment is momentous. It is a cause for celebration. Couples usually wish to share this declaration of their love and commitment with family and friends.

The celebration. Some couples celebrate their wedding in lavish style while others mark it in a more modest way. But no matter how you organise your wedding, the core issue is that you make a lifelong commitment to one another. Once you become husband and wife, you have embarked on a unique journey together. From now on, you will share your lives in a most intimate way; you are next of kin to one another; you are on the same team. No more soul-searching and the heartache of trying to find a soulmate – your soulmate is here at your side as you walk down the aisle together and go out to create your future lives.

What the researchers tell us. From the many facts and figures on marriage vying for our attention, the evidence to support the married state is both conclusive and convincing. In essence, research indicates that married people have:

- Greater relationship satisfaction – feeling happier

- Higher levels of relationship commitment – feeling more confident

- Higher levels of relationship stability – feeling more rooted

- Better mental and physical health – feeling fitter and living longer

- Fewer depressive symptoms – feeling calmer

- Higher levels of trust and intimacy – feeling more fulfilled, when compared to their unmarried peers.

I hope this makes you feel even happier about your decision to get married.

WHAT IS LOVE?

The Oxford English Dictionary defines love as – *An intense feeling of deep affection or fondness for a person or thing.* Love is a special emotional bond that attaches us to one another. Our brains are hardwired to need love, hardwired by millions of years of evolution.

Love is, in fact, a survival imperative. Babies need love so that they can develop and grow, just as much as they need nourishment and shelter. Indeed, the brain codes isolation and abandonment as danger, and the touch and emotional response of a loved one as safety.

No doubt you and your partner are enjoying those intense feelings – the excitement of hearing that special voice, the thrill of receiving that loving message, the joyful anticipation of proclaiming your love for each other on your wedding day.

How did you fall in love?

Let's take a quick look at how you fell in love with your partner. Were you *swept off your feet*? Were you *blown away*? Did you *fall madly in love* from the start? These expressions, frequently used to describe initial attraction, have one thing in common. They are actions that happened *to* you. They sound as if you were the passive victim, helpless to control your own feelings and reactions at the time.

And maybe that's exactly how it felt for you. Indeed, such highly charged emotional experiences can and do happen. When they happen, it feels very exciting. You fall, are blown away or swept off on a wave of emotion. These are passive, spontaneous responses to arousal. They require no effort from you.

But, as your relationship develops, you don't just continue to react blindly to those wonderful feelings. You start to think about them, analyse them and finally own them. You learn to become more proactive in your relationship with your partner. Now, your love can progress and deepen.

However, not all deep and lasting relationships start this way. Maybe you did not experience a great rush of emotion for your partner at the start. Maybe your love grew slowly over time. Perhaps, initially, the attraction was not mutual – one of you did the running, the other had to be wooed.

The emotional pattern that you felt at the start of your relationship has no real significance. What is important is that you are both attracted to one another now, that you feel happy and comfortable when you are together and that you feel that your connection is deepening.

CAN THIS LOVE LAST?

Did you ever wonder if what you are experiencing right now is too good to be real and lasting? Do you worry that your love for one another will diminish and become jaded with time – that familiarity will erode the excitement and passion that you feel now?

There are two possible answers to this question.

Answer 1 – Romantic love cannot last.

There is a school of thought that argues that romantic feelings fade with time. Some people fear that what is now new and exciting will become predictable and all too familiar as time goes on. Indeed, the heightened feelings and euphoria experienced at the start of a relationship do mellow and deepen with time. If you have been carried away on a wave of ecstatic feelings, at some stage, your feet will touch ground again.

But what proponents of this philosophy fail to see is the growing wonder and excitement of a deeper, lasting love. Having your feet touch the ground does not mean the end of excitement. For as love mellows and matures, those intense feelings can develop into a passionate bond between you. And this bond is strengthened by a growing mutual respect and trust. The key is to recognise the healthy feeling of deep happiness and connection, as well as the excitement of infatuation.

Can you recall the first kiss with your partner? Can you recall the second and the third?

Chances are you cannot recall each kiss in order. The first kiss was a new experience. But that does not mean that subsequent kisses have not been exciting. No doubt some kisses have made it into your memory bank – associated with special events or experiences. But the unremembered kisses have still contributed to building up the bond between you.

So, too with romantic love. There will of course be moments that are more memorable and exciting than others. But your continuing love for one another runs deeper – like an underground river, not always seen but constantly there.

Answer 2 – Romantic love can and does last.

Let's start by addressing the argument above that romantic love will fade with time. Familiarity breeds contempt, they say. But how about familiarity breeding contentment instead? Why should familiarity be considered a negative? Think of the calm and soothing feeling of being with your beloved. When you are with your partner, I hope that you can feel relaxed, fully yourself. Together, you are going to create a new space or home – both materially, physically, and emotionally, or metaphorically. It is there, in your own comfortable place, which only you two share, that your love will thrive and blossom.

The two key words in Answer 1 are **NEW and EXCITING**. Why not resolve now to keep that newness and excitement in your relationship? After all, life is full of change. We must keep changing if we are to develop. The challenge is to stay as fully aware of one another as you can. Watch out for taking each other for granted – keep going out on dates; surprise one another; do little acts of kindness for each other. All this will help keep your relationship alive and vital.

Programmed to last. The other significant point is this – the romantic love you are experiencing now is designed to last. Why? Because for us, as humans, romantic love is an essential part of our survival programming. It's in our genes. Yes, we humans have a wired-in need for connection. We are born with innate needs for comfort, sustenance and soothing. Above all, we need an emotional bond with another human. It is this bond that helps keep romance alive

From child... When you were a child your parents were there to meet your emotional needs. We know that love is a survival imperative. As we know, babies need love in order to develop and grow. You were dependent on your parents to give you care and nurturing. The attachments formed with the important people in your life as a child helped you feel secure and confident in yourself as an individual. As you grew up, that sense of self grew too. You gradually weaned yourself from emotional dependence on your parents. You discovered your own autonomy and developed your own identity.

To adult... Now, as an adult, you hopefully still feel connected to, but no longer dependent on your parents. You can maybe see them as friends and equals. You have established your own life and identity. You have matured and found a mate, a companion for life, a sexual partner with whom you may have children. Together, you two form a new social entity – a couple with an emotional bond that will grow stronger over time.

John Bowlby, the psychologist who developed the Theory of Attachment, tells us that lovers are connected by a neural net. When tuned in emotionally, lovers help each other reach a physical and emotional balance that promotes optimal functioning. So that is what you and your partner will hopefully achieve – each of you will allow the other to become your best selves.

Romance deepens with time. When you get married you set out on a journey together. You may think that you already know one another well. But the beauty of commitment and marriage is that you have a whole lifetime ahead of you in which to get to know one another more fully. The wedding day is just the start. From now on, you will be able to explore your own potential in the knowledge that you have the support and love of your spouse.

REFLECTION

Why have you and your fiancé(e) decided to get married?
Sit down separately and address these questions. You may want to just think through your responses but writing down

your answers can be helpful. Some people use a notebook – real or virtual, specifically for these exercises.

a) What does the word **marriage** mean to you? Think about this – think way beyond your wedding day. What is your vision for the two of you into the future?

b) What are the **three most important reasons** for you to get married?

c) If you were to summarise your **hopes and expectations** for your marriage, what would you say? Write down a few thoughts – think of images, ideas, imagined scenarios and feelings.

Feedback

Now share your answers with each other. Even the act of speaking aloud your reasons for getting married can help you realise the implications of this important decision.

See where you think alike. Similar hopes and dreams are great. Are you excited by your partner's ideas and vision? If necessary, ask your partner to clarify their expectations, explaining what they mean.

What about the differences?

In what areas are your visions different? It is good to be challenged by another way of seeing things, another attitude to life. Can you open your mind to accepting and embracing a new way of thinking? Be curious, not furious, about this insight into your partner.

At this time of heightened sensibilities, couples sometimes allow small differences to become big dramas. Of course, it is reassuring when you think alike on fundamental issues, but wouldn't life be dull indeed if you agreed on everything? In fact, it is important, at this stage of your relationship, to figure out a way to handle differences or disagreements. See *When Couples Differ* – No. 1 in the Troubleshooting Guide (p. 108).

CONCLUSION

What matters ultimately is that you both agree on the fundamentals of what marriage is all about. And remember that romantic love, the wonderful feeling of being in love, can and will last and thrive once it is shared and nurtured.

Together you two can build on the love you already have. As the years move on, may your love grow and mature into a wonderful, strong and beautiful bond.

Chapter 2
Who Am I?

Married love, like all love, requires giving, sharing of oneself. True. However, giving of oneself does not mean ignoring the self. Before you can truly give to another, you must be comfortable with who you are. What are your values and priorities; what are your needs? To recognise what your needs are requires a degree of insight and self-awareness. Once your own needs are met, the relationship with another person will have a stable foundation. It is good to remember that you cannot fully love someone else until you have learned to love and accept yourself.

So, who are you and what are your needs?

Let's start with your identity; who you think you are. We are all products of our life experiences. Our self-image is based on what we perceive as reflected back to us by others, from the time we were very little right up to today. Our sense of self is also informed by how secure we felt in our attachments to the important people in our lives as we grew up. These attachments are models for how we form relationships as adults.

WHO AM I QUIZ

Do you feel that you know who you really are? Can you understand why your partner loves you? Answer the questions below and find out more about yourself.

1) Describe how you most often felt as a child in relation to your family.

2) Can you recall two or three family rules, either spoken or implied, when you were growing up?

3) Who was the person you most trusted as a child?

4) How did you feel about yourself as a teenager?

5) Name three of your good qualities.

6) What change would you most like to make in yourself?

7) When you see yourself in the mirror, how do you usually feel?

8) What do you most appreciate about your relationship with your fiancé(e)?

9) Name two situations in which you feel really contented and at ease.

10) Name two qualities that you value most highly in others.

CONSIDERING THE OUTCOME

Looking back at your childhood can be quite telling. Consider the role you played in your family growing up – happy child, carer, coper, scapegoat, clown… Is the role you took on then reflected now in your adult relationship? Think about this. Are you comfortable to play that role again or would you like to see a different dynamic in your relationship with your partner?

Now look at the messages you took from your childhood in relation to your view of yourself. Has that self-image changed now that you have matured into adulthood?

To what extent has your philosophy or outlook on life been influenced by your family of origin? Have you rejected some messages and accepted others? It is good to process these influences and decide what you want to adopt and claim as your own.

When you look back at your teenage years, how do you feel you coped with peer pressure? Did you get somewhat swallowed up by mass culture? Are you happy with the adult that has emerged from those years?

There are usually aspects of ourselves that we would like to change. And being aware of that is important. Staying open to change means that you are really alive. It means that you can imagine things being different, that you are open to new possibilities.

I hope that you had no difficulty in naming your good qualities. If you are reluctant to claim your positive attributes, stop and think. You are a good person, so recognise that fact. Being kind to yourself, acknowledging your good qualities means that you are then better able to reach out to and love others.

I also hope that you are happy with the person you see when you look in the mirror. You are beautiful, unique and your fiancé(e) loves you. If you tend to think that being aware of your personal attributes is somehow self-indulgent, please see *Self-Centred v Self-Assured* below.

Regarding the final three questions of the quiz, these are designed to make you more aware of what you've got – to recognise the beauty of being in a loving relationship, to appreciate what makes you happy and to admire the good in others.

If you would like to explore getting to know yourself more fully, see *Johari Window* – No. 2 in the Troubleshooting Guide (p. 109).

Self-Centred v Self-Assured

Do you feel comfortable when asked to acknowledge your own good qualities? Can you allow your strengths make you feel happy about yourself? Liking and accepting yourself should not be confused with being self-centred. If you think that it is somehow wrong to love and accept yourself, let me tell you, it is not.

The self-centred person is one whose behaviour is motivated by insecurity or a chronic need for reassurance. Self-centred people think constantly about themselves. They find it difficult to identify or empathise with another person's needs or desires. The self-centred person looks inwards, not outwards.

Think of it this way. If you are unhappy with yourself, if you are constantly critical of yourself, you will constantly seek reassurance from others. You become preoccupied with what others think of you. You will be inclined to take offence at the slightest perceived insult, even when this is not intended. If you are unhappy with yourself, you will also be less likely to enjoy the beauty of the world around you, to notice other people's needs, to smile. For with so much focus on self, how can you reach out openly to someone else?

The self-assured person, on the other hand, is someone who does not worry so much about how he/she is perceived by others. Self-assurance means self-acceptance. Once you are happy enough within yourself, you can start to look outwards, start to think of others. You become aware of the needs and feelings of those around you. You are concerned for their welfare and happiness. Because you are looking outwards, you are open to appreciate life – the singing of the birds, the beauty of the breeze as it rustles through the trees; the little things that we can all fail to notice at times. And this appreciation, in turn, makes you happier.

Helping yourself to feel happy has the added effect of bringing joy to those around you. So, reassure yourself; allow yourself to accept and enjoy the unique gifts that you possess.

NEEDS AND EXPECTATIONS

What are your ***needs*** in this relationship? Think about this – write down a few thoughts if you like. Then consider the list below:

1. to be touched

2. to be held

3. to be comforted

4. to feel attached

5. to feel loved

6. to be allowed to be myself

7. to feel accepted for who I am

8. to feel comfortable to own and express my deepest thoughts

Read through your list. Are your needs being met in this relationship? Are there some areas where you would like to see change? What about your partner? Share your thoughts on this.

Now what about *expectations*?

Have you ever had an experience like the following?

A friend whom you don't know very well asks you to a party. Friday night, 7 pm. All sorted. You look forward to the evening, planning what to wear, wondering who else will be there.

Friday night arrives and you head out, all dressed up and hungry. After all, the invitation was for 7 pm so there will certainly be food.

You are the first person to arrive. The apartment is tiny, but sparsely furnished. You offer to help and are assigned to open some bottles of wine and beer.

Finally, well after 8 pm, others begin to arrive. The place soon fills up. You are busy serving drinks. Suddenly, it is 10 pm. and you realise that you are starving. You spot a basket of potato crisps on the windowsill, but by the time you get there, only a few crumbs remain.

You overhear someone say, "Food? No. Never at Mark's. We always eat before we come here."

That answers it. The invitation was to a party, but you had assumed that food would be served. You had visualised a different type of party. Others who were invited had different expectations. They ate before they came.
No one is to blame here. The fact is that if you had clarified with Mark at the time of the invitation, you would have known better what to expect.

Moral? Check out and clarify before commitment.

This is obviously a petty incident. But it highlights the importance of naming and sharing your expectations when it comes to the very important question of marriage.

REFLECTION

Can you name some of your **expectations** of being married to your partner?

If you run out of ideas, check the list below:

- Life will be much happier than it is now
- I will feel more secure in myself
- We will continue to go out on date nights
- I will still be able to go out with my friends at least once a week
- We will have separate bank accounts
- We will have a joint bank account
- We will share our money equally
- We will have two children
- We will live abroad for a while
- We will go away for holidays together every year
- We will settle down near my parents
- I will be the main earner

- I will continue with my career, even if that means frequent trips abroad

- My spouse will stay at home when we have children

When you have completed your lists, share them with one another.

Has this exercise made you more aware of your own expectations of married life? You have probably already discussed many of these issues with your partner. But there may be some ideas that you have not shared. By becoming more aware of each other's vision of your life together, you can build a united and solid foundation for your marriage. Once again, remember that it is all about communication.

INVESTING IN YOURSELF

During this exciting time of preparing for your marriage, it is important to reserve some time for yourself – time to check into your deeper feelings, time to unwind, time to feel free.

Whether you go for a walk on your own, go to the gym or simply give yourself an IT-free evening at home, you will benefit from having some time for reflection.

Take the pulse of your general health and feelings:

- Are you getting enough sleep? Sleep deprivation can lead to mood fluctuations and general irritability.

- Are you eating a healthy diet? No fad or extreme diets allowed. Eating healthily will help you feel more energised and happier with yourself.

- Are you generally pleased with how your wedding preparations are going? If you feel there is too much to be done, see *Feeling Overwhelmed – Using the Triage Method* – No. 3 in the Troubleshooting Guide (p. 111).

- Have you delegated responsibility for certain tasks to reliable others? If not, why not start now. Your friends and family are usually very happy to be of help.

- Do you think that you and your fiancé(e) are getting enough down time together? If not, factor that in.

- Have any issues arisen recently that have caused you to feel upset? If so, see *Feeling Unexpectedly Upset* – No. 4 in the Troubleshooting Guide (p. 113).

CONCLUSION

I hope that you now feel more comfortable with the unique person who is you. I hope that you are happy within yourself. Remember, you are wonderful, beautiful, unique, and special. You are much loved by so many people and most especially loved by your fiancé(e).

That is surely a cause for joy.

Chapter 3
Who Are You?
Knowing Your Partner

Isn't it fun being in love? I hope that you are really excited by the thought of being married to your partner. The aim of this chapter is to enable you to take time to stop and think about the person with whom you are planning to share the rest of your life.

How long have you two known each other? If you have been together for a few years, chances are that you feel that you know each other very well. But how well? Consider the reflection below to find out. There are no right or wrong answers, so be honest and open.

KNOWING MY PARTNER QUIZ

1. Name three qualities that you most admire in your partner.

2. What is it that first attracted you to your partner?

3. How did your relationship develop – fast, slowly, in fits and starts…?

4. Can you recall your first date with your partner?

5. Have you had any periods of separation since your relationship developed?

6. If so, what were the causes?

7. What interests do you both share?

8. What priorities and values do you and your partner have in common?

9. What ambitions does your partner have?

10. Do you differ on any issue which one of you considers important?

11. What are your partner's greatest fears?

12. How easily does your partner express his/her feelings?

13. Have you witnessed your partner getting angry?

14. Are you happy with the way your partner deals with his/her anger?

15. What causes your partner to feel stressed?

16. How does your partner manage stress?

17. How good is your partner's general health?

18. Is there anything about your partner that turns you off?

19. If you were to ask your partner to make one change in behaviour or attitude, what would it be?

20. What has been your most romantic experience together so far?

Now swap notes with your partner. It is good to know which of your qualities your partner most admires. It is always fun to recall your first date together and review the story of your romance. Some of the issues raised here may give rise to a more detailed discussion. That is good – it gives each of you further knowledge of and insight into the other.

Some questions may reveal areas where one of you feels more comfortable or confident than the other – perhaps in the way you handle stress or deal with feelings. If so, see if you can help each other, by listening carefully and accepting that there is much to be gained by having an open mind.

This is just the start of your life journey of discovery together. Remember, most of us do not know ourselves very well, so it is not surprising that there is much more to be discovered about your fiancé(e).

IT IS OK TO DISAGREE

If there are areas of disagreement that are important to either of you, why not think about addressing them now? Don't wait. The issues that bother you now will not go away once you are married. If you tend to think that by ignoring a problem, it will somehow disappear, then sit up and take note. Issues left unresolved can simmer away under the surface, but only for a while. So, address these issues now and prevent them from developing in significance.

No two people agree on everything. In fact, it is a sign of a healthy relationship if each of you feels comfortable enough to express your own opinions and thoughts even when they are very different from those expressed by your partner. What is significant, however, is what happens when disagreements occur. *See Chapter Seven – Confrontation.*

SECRECY v PRIVACY

How open is your relationship with your fiancé(e)? Are there aspects of yourself or of your past life that you have not shared with your partner? It is good, at this point, to look at the distinction between secrecy and privacy.

Secrecy is something that you withhold. You want to keep certain information to yourself. Perhaps you have grown up with a particular secret. You have become used to withholding information from others.

If this is the case, now that you are about to take on a life partner is a good time to review your secret or secrets. For if your loving relationship is to be as open as possible, there should be no secrets between you.

Privacy is something that you give. You respect your partner's right to privacy and allow him/her to share with you in their own time. This may require patience on your part.

If you are aware of some hidden aspect of your partner's life that you would like to know more fully, what can you do about it? Firstly, you need to build up trust. Your partner must feel comfortable to risk sharing with you. He/she needs to know that you will respect the confidentiality of their secrets. You are there with a listening and caring ear, ready to give your support.

And what about your secrets? Are you prepared to share your secrets with your partner, in the knowledge that they will be treated with confidentiality? Talk about this. The two of you are embarking on a new life together, independent of extended family and friends. You both need to draw a new boundary, one that respects the intimate details that only you two can share.

If you are used to sharing the intimate details of your life with your parents, your siblings, or your friends, it will require some practice to change that behaviour pattern. But it is really important to do so. Remember that from now on your spouse will be your nearest and dearest, your teammate and life partner. Start today to create your own safe box of intimacy, not to be shared with extended family and friends.

I WANT TO LOOK INSIDE YOUR HEAD

Getting to really know someone can take a lifetime. The psychologists tell us that we can never truly know another person – in fact, most of us never fully know even ourselves. At the core of each of us there lies a secret and hidden self that is quite difficult to access.

But having accepted the challenge of coming to terms with our true selves, we can appreciate more fully the challenge and indeed the privilege of getting really close to our loved one.

For both of you, no doubt there are certain aspects of one another that still remain a mystery. Maybe it concerns what one of you regards as an illogical reaction to something quite simple. Is there a story there? Does it relate back to a childhood experience?

Maybe you are already aware of your partner's reluctance to discuss a particular issue. Do you have any No-Go areas – certain topics that you are reluctant to discuss with your partner?

Perhaps you tried to confide in your partner before, and things became uncomfortable or unpleasant. So rather than continue the conversation, it was dropped and has lain low ever since.

But there may be times when you become vaguely aware of a little hump, a little hint of something lying between you. It is just a small issue, you might think, but it has significance. Otherwise, why does it keep slinking back into your mind?

Why not make this the subject of a Listening Exercise? *See Chapter Five.* Take it in turns to be speaker A. Listen carefully to what your partner has to say.

Does this help answer some of your questions? You might even get to laugh at how simple the issue appears now that you have discussed it together.

THE PSYCHOLOGICAL CONTRACT

From the moment we start a relationship with another person, we form a series of opinions about them, along with expectations about how they will behave or what attitudes they have. Based on our initial impressions, we formulate a contract in our heads with them.

This one-sided contract is also informed by our own needs – maybe a need for someone strong to protect us; or a need to bond with someone who is able to articulate feelings because we find that difficult.

Once we have found a partner who seems to meet our needs, we expect them to behave accordingly.

How do we form our impressions of other people? Our opinions and perceptions are based largely on our experience to date. Children who feel loved and cared for will be trusting of others unless they have been taught about stranger danger. So, too, we accept others according to our life experiences.

INTERPRETATION OF REALITY

Consider this – four people are walking down the road when a cat, unknown to any of them, comes towards them.

One person thinks – *What a gorgeous cat. I'd love him as a pet.*

The next person thinks – *A cat like that would be great at keeping mice out of the house.*

The third person thinks – *What a great photo opportunity. I'll capture that cute cat on camera.*

The fourth person thinks – *Get me out of here. That's a dangerous-looking animal. I know someone who was bitten and scratched by a cat like that and nearly died.*

The important point here is that the cat has not changed – it is still the same cat. What does differ is the way it is seen or perceived by each of the observers. And each observer is, in turn, informed by his or her prior experience, cultural background and family of origin. So, which of the four sees the real cat? Is there a definitive reality?

Our perception of others often reveals more about ourselves and our own life experiences than about the other. We see things not so much as they are, but as we are.

MANAGING OUR EXPECTATIONS

Have you ever been surprised by the way your partner reacted or acted in a certain situation? If so, just think about it again. To what extent did your surprise stem from your own preconceived notions of your partner? Perhaps you had never articulated these expectations. Therefore, your partner was unaware of this one-sided, unspoken contract. How did you address the issue at the time? Can you learn anything from this experience?

It is important to be aware of and manage our expectations. If they are not communicated, and our partner fails to behave in the way we expect, then it is not surprising that we are disappointed, and they are taken aback by our reaction.

CONCLUSION

As you can see, getting to know your partner is an ongoing, lifelong experience. With good communication, your knowledge and appreciation of one another will grow. There will be wonderful insights and challenges ahead. The important thing is that you continue to love one another and that you feel comfortable together.

Chapter 4
Building a Healthy Relationship

Before we discuss the essential elements to building a healthy relationship, it is worth seeing where your relationship is at present. Look at the five stages outlined below. Where would you place your relationship at the moment? Remember that it can take a long time to reach stages four and five. But it is good to be aware of the challenges and struggles couples must go through in order to build a sound and steadfast bond.

RELATIONSHIP STAGES

1. **In love with being in love.** This describes the wonderful feeling of euphoria experienced when you fall in love – remember what I said earlier about falling? You can get swept up on a wave of thrilling emotions. Because it feels so exciting, some people are reluctant to move on and allow their relationships to deepen.

   You probably know some of those serial romantics. They are madly in love with a different person every few weeks. They have in fact become so addicted to the adrenalin rush that they abandon a relationship once things settle down.

   But if a relationship is to deepen and last, it must progress to the next stage.

Power adjustment. As two individuals become a couple, adjustments are inevitable. Who is in charge? Each of you is faced with the challenge of deciding what compromises you are willing to make as you create a new life together. Can you form a partnership without relinquishing your independence and autonomy?

An effective image here is the seesaw. It is difficult to keep completely level with one another when on a seesaw. At any given time, one person is higher than the other. When you are high, you feel on top of the world. When you are low you realise what you are losing by being in this relationship. This is when rows can start.

The challenge here is to ensure that neither partner is consistently on top. If that happens, the seesaw is no longer fulfilling its function. It is designed to move up and down, to keep each of you loving more consciously while you adjust to growing together.

2. **Maturing love.** As your love matures, it stabilises. By this stage, you will have dealt with most of the power struggles and you are able to see more clearly how you can operate effectively as a couple. You can acknowledge one another's strengths. This makes each of you feel validated by the other.

You will know that your love has matured when each of you realises that your partner has become the first person to whom you turn when seeking comfort or reassurance.

3. **Acceptance of each other as you are.** When your relationship reaches this stage, it is truly a liberating experience. You no longer play mind games with each other. You now feel totally comfortable to be

yourself around your partner. It also means that you accept your partner for who he/she is. Your love for one another is no longer a qualified love:

e.g. *I'll love you more when I've changed you into the person I want you to be.*

4. **Equilibrium.** When you achieve this final stage, you've arrived. You are a team. The element of competition or subtle vying for control has diminished. You feel happy and comfortable in your partner's company. Being together brings out the best in each of you. The seesaw is now operating effectively – playing to your strengths. You now see your partner as the person most qualified to help you grow and become your best self.

Of course, the stages outlined here are not definitive. Every relationship develops in its own way and at its own pace. There can be setbacks along the way. It is not unusual to revisit the power adjustment issue several times. But the key points remain valid no matter what the relationship pattern. So, talk to your partner – where does each of you see the relationship now?

BUILDING A SOLID RELATIONSHIP – ESSENTIAL ELEMENTS

Building a healthy relationship is like building a house. There are certain ingredients that are essential – a solid foundation, walls, windows; and others that are optional extras – skylights, underfloor heating, solar panels. We now look at what I regard as essential ingredients. Read the list below and see what you think. Are there some other elements that you and your partner feel should be added to the list?

1. ATTRACTION

What attracted you to your partner? Are you aware of a special chemistry between you? At a subconscious, as well as conscious, level we are programmed to seek a mate who has the characteristics we consider important for procreation. It is part of the master plan for the continuation of the human species.

No doubt, this is not what you thought at a conscious level when you were first attracted to your partner. You were probably more aware of your own physical response – arousal, excitement, joy at seeing each other and being together.

REFLECTION

Which personality traits attracted you to your partner?

What do you most enjoy about being together? It is good to stop and think about this. Then communicate your feelings to one another.

What does your partner find most attractive in you? Discuss. It feels good to know that you are attractive.

2. BEING IN TUNE

John Bowlby, the psychologist who first recognised the different types of attachment in relationships states:

When tuned in emotionally, lovers help each other reach a physical and emotional balance that promotes optimal functioning.

How emotionally tuned in to your partner are you? Can you recognise when he/she is upset? If so, can you identify the underlying feeling? Sometimes it helps if you can suggest an emotion that your partner may not be willing or able to name.

REFLECTION

Do you feel that your partner understands and accepts you for who you are? Are you comfortable to express what you feel? Do you sometimes play along just to keep the peace?

What does your partner think? Resolve to listen respectfully to one another and not to take differences personally. Don't be afraid to say what you feel. Each of you is entitled to name your own thoughts and emotions.

3. MUTUAL RESPECT

Do you respect your partner? Do you feel respected by your partner? What does the word RESPECT mean to you? The Oxford dictionary defines respect as showing regard or esteem; being considerate and appreciative. Does that sound like the way you and your partner treat one another?

Are there times when you show a lack of respect for your partner? Can you identify when this occurs? What provokes the change in attitude – your own mood, your partner's behaviour or something else? If there are times when you think that there is a lack of respect between you, talk to your partner about it.

REFLECTION

Admiration breeds respect. Can you name three aspects or qualities in your partner that you really admire? Tell each other. Naming what you most admire in one another adds to the mutual respect you feel.

4. TRUST

This is such a powerful quality. When we trust we have a confident expectation, we feel that we can rely on someone to behave or react in an honourable way. Trust is a first cousin of respect. Once we feel respect for someone, we in turn want to behave in a way that honours that relationship – we want to be trustworthy.

Building trust takes time and consistency. As you and your partner have got to know each other, over time, your confidence in one another has also grown. Consistency here refers to behaviour and attitudes that are not erratic but are dependable and reliable. As you have become more familiar with your partner's behaviour pattern, I hope that your trust in him/her has grown.

REFLECTION

Maybe there are times when you feel that you would like to know more about a certain aspect of your partner. Perhaps it is an issue from their past, or it may relate to something that occurred recently. Most likely when you explore this, there will be nothing to cause you concern, but if you have a niggling doubt or question that will not go away, it needs to be addressed. See *When Trust Issues Arise* – No. 5 in the Troubleshooting Guide (p. 114).

5. BALANCE

In a healthy relationship between two adults, no one person should be constantly in charge. Who is in charge in your relationship? Is it run as a democracy or a dictatorship? How do you feel about that? And how does your partner feel? Do you experience a sneaking resentment from time to time that your opinion is not taken into consideration, or that somehow your feelings don't count? If so, then it is time to discuss this with your partner. Don't make the mistake of ignoring your gut feeling, hoping that everything will be better after you are married.

Or maybe, your partner feels that you are always in charge. Maybe he/she is hesitant to voice any resentment at present. But if resentment is there, it will only build up unless it is dealt with. Talk about it.

REFLECTION

If you feel there is an imbalance in your relationship, this is the time to readjust it so that you both enter marriage feeling happy and comfortable. Don't be afraid to address this issue – there is no room for fear of one another in a healthy and happy relationship. Think of that seesaw image.

RELATIONSHIP ROLES

At this important stage of your relationship, it is worth looking at the communication pattern you have developed.

When you and your partner are discussing something that you consider serious, or when you are having a disagreement, how do you mostly feel?

1. Like a child being spoken to by a parent?

2. Like a parent speaking to a child?

3. Like an adult talking to another adult?

It is good to recognise the games we sometimes play:

- The **child** accepts no responsibility for his/her behaviour. The child can be sulky or spoilt; petulant or demanding. He/she will wriggle out of being held accountable. In the child's eyes, the problem is usually someone else's fault. Thus, the child can be quite controlling in a subtle way.

- The **parent** holds the high moral ground. He/she thinks that the other partner can do nothing without their permission. Control, here, is more blatant, and acquiescence is expected. The parent does not see the need for compromise or negotiation, yet becomes upset when the other baulks at his/her imperious demands.

- The **adult** acknowledges the rights of the other to have their own feelings and to hold different opinions. The adult listens carefully and reflects on what their partner thinks and feels. When two adults discuss a problem issue, they can reach agreement or compromise, with each feeling respected and heard. When a resolution is reached, adults will review the incident and learn from it.

REFLECTION

If you were to describe your role in this relationship with your partner in the terms outlined above, what would it be? Perhaps you recognise yourself in different roles – sometimes playing the innocent and irresponsible child; sometimes the bossy and controlling parent; and also, at times, the mature, respectful, and calm adult. It is good here to consider the following:

- The tone of voice you use – does it get shrill or petulant at times?

- Your body language – do you sometimes wag a finger at your partner, or shrug or roll your eyes when he/she is speaking?

- Your choice of words – do you tend to exaggerate certain details or use emotive language?

CONCLUSION

The happiest and healthiest relationships are built on mutual respect, trust, and love. With care and attention, these grow and deepen over time. Now that you are aware of the essential elements, you will, no doubt, be better prepared to build a wonderful relationship together.

Chapter 5
Communication

Numerous researchers, including Byers and Demmons, 1999; Carrere & Gottman, 1999; Christensin & Shenk, 1991, have identified effective communication between partners as a vital component of overall relationship satisfaction.

Indeed, several surveys conducted by mental health professionals, academics, lawyers and the media reveal that poor communication is the most common factor leading to marriage breakdown.

When you think about it, this is easy to understand. After all, we spend a great part of our lives trying to understand others or trying to get them to understand us. If we knew how other people thought and felt, life would be so much simpler.

How well do you and your partner communicate?

At the moment, you may feel so much in love that you think you know what the other is feeling.

- *I don't need to ask Mary how her day has been. I just know by looking at her.*
  or
- *Paul always knows when I'm upset. He just has to hold me, and I feel better.*

And it is true. Sometimes being touched or held in a loving way speaks louder than any words. Our body language and actions can communicate quite effectively. But there are also times when it is important and necessary to speak – to find the words to express your thoughts and feelings.

What about fundamental issues? Do you have worries or concerns that are left unspoken? How brave or comfortable are you when it comes to talking to your partner about an issue on which you don't agree?

THREE ELEMENTS OF COMMUNICATION

1. COMMUNICATING THE MESSAGE

There are so many ways of communication, some more subtle than others.

NON-VERBAL

No doubt you and your partner have already developed a secret code of non-verbal communication – a nod, a wink, a facial expression that conveys a great deal. It is fun and exciting to be understood so easily by your beloved.

We also communicate by our behaviour – just think of kissing, cuddling, doing little acts of kindness for one another.

Of course, as with other forms of communication, non-verbal messages are not always positive. Think of sighing, sulking, and stonewalling – that awful gulf of silence which can be a cruel weapon.

REFLECTION

What do you tend to do if you feel annoyed or frustrated with your partner?

VERBAL When it comes to verbal communication, it is important to choose words that express your message as accurately as possible. This can be quite a challenge at times. But here are a few guidelines:

- Stop and think before you speak – then speak with respect. No insults.

- Ask a question rather than make an accusation – e.g. *Did you remember to collect the clothes from the cleaners?* Not, *don't tell me you forgot the clothes again!*

- Identify your dominant feeling. It is good to note that anger is usually a secondary emotion, masking another feeling, e.g. hurt, loneliness, sadness. Try to access your primary, underlying emotion.

- Name your feelings rather than label your partner e.g. *I am really disappointed that you forgot,* not, *You're so forgetful,* or, *You're hopeless.*

- Keep things in perspective. Being able to triage situations is a great skill. Wait a little, then ask yourself – *How important is this issue to me?*

- Make a request rather than issue a command. This is a most effective way of getting your message across. *Can you please…?* works much better than, *Give me the…* Orders and commands are coercive and therefore are often met with resistance, while a gentle request can be more persuasive.

2. GETTING THE MESSAGE: LISTENING

Mastering the art of true Listening is, in my experience, one of the greatest challenges in any relationship. Full attention is needed if we are to really hear the message. Try following the exercise below with your partner.

Warning – this is not as easy as it reads and will require practice.

LISTENING EXERCISE – listening is a highly important skill. It requires real concentration and focus on what you are hearing.

- Choose an issue that has bothered you and could become contentious. Agree on who gets to speak first – Speaker A.

- Speaker A tells his/her story. When speaking, focus not only on practical details, but also on what you were **feeling** at the time,
  e.g. *When that happened, I felt…*

- Speaker B must listen attentively as A is speaking. **Do not interrupt**, even if you disagree with what is being said.

- When A has finished speaking, B **gives feedback**. Feedback here does not mean giving your reaction. It means simply feeding back what has been said. Start with,
  What I have heard you say is…
  Stick to what you have heard. Report on the feelings A has articulated. Avoid adding in your own comments.

- Once B has given the feedback, allow A to **correct** if necessary. Perhaps you omitted some details that he/she considers important.

- **Reflect**. Now that you have heard your partner's story, what do you think? How do you feel? Are you

less concerned or more? Are there still unanswered questions for you? Ask your partner for further clarification if you think it is needed,
e.g., *What did you mean when you said...?*

- When Speaker A feels that the message has been truly heard, reverse the roles. This time, the listener gets to talk. You can choose the same issue, recounting it from your perspective, or choose another issue. Again, focus on your feelings when this event took place.

- As before, B cannot interrupt or correct what is being said – there will be time for that later. B simply listens attentively so that he/she can recount what A has said as accurately as possible.

- Continue to follow the steps as before, giving feedback that focuses on the feelings experienced by A, allowing A to correct if necessary.

- Once both of you have spoken, check how you feel. Does each of you feel heard?

- What was it like to replay the tape, saying:
  What I have heard you say is that when I did/said...you felt hurt/sad/frustrated...?
  It is quite a powerful experience; I think you will agree.

3. ACCEPTING THE MESSAGE

If mastering the art of truly listening takes some practice, this stage requires lots of self-awareness. Whether or not you realise it, your life experience to date has given you certain fixed ideas. These, in turn, effect the judgements and assumptions you make.

We apply filters to much of what we hear. These filters are formed from our own experiences, our culture and background. They are particularly handy when we hear a message that we don't want to accept. Maybe it is a negative comment or implied criticism. If we are not prepared for such negativity, we apply the denial filter:

- *That can't be true*

- *He/she doesn't really mean it*

- *There is some mistake here*

This form of wishful thinking is an effective self-protection mechanism. The trouble is, however, that it prevents us from getting to know ourselves more fully. We miss the chance of gaining insight into our blind spot – see *Johari Window* – No. 2 in the Troubleshooting Guide (p. 109).

Now that you have found a loving partner, it is important to be open to accepting his/her messages, even if they sometimes make for uncomfortable listening. Perhaps it is a matter of trusting that this is an opportunity to see how your words, attitude or behaviour can impact on those you love.

It is not only the denial filter that impedes us from getting or accepting the message. Our previous experiences can cause us to make judgments or assumptions that colour our interpretation of reality. A certain phrase or tone of voice can evoke a situation in the past where we felt uncomfortable or under pressure, so we respond by becoming defensive.

REFLECTION

It is good to try always to be open to receiving the message. If what we hear is not what we expected to hear, avoid denial or defensiveness. Be curious; ask for clarification; be ready to accept that we are not always right.

If you tend to become unexpectedly upset if you encounter any negative feedback, see *Feeling Unexpectedly Upset* – No. 4 in the Troubleshooting Guide (p. 113).

ACHIEVING EFFECTIVE AND CLEAR COMMUNICATION

This is the greatest challenge in any relationship and especially in marriage. To communicate effectively with one another requires constant attention to detail. Be sure to articulate what is important to you so that your partner is in no doubt. See the Case Study below.

Case Study – Peter and Jenny

Peter and Jenny have been together for six years and have recently got engaged. Jenny had been waiting and hoping for Peter to commit to their relationship and propose getting married. And when he finally commits, he does it in style – on a gondola in Venice. Jenny is overjoyed.

During the past six years, there have been a number of issues that threatened to cause tension between them. But Jenny would do anything to avoid confrontation. She has usually managed to steer the conversation onto a more neutral topic to avoid an argument.

One of these issues is the question of children. Jenny really wants to have a family, but she has discovered that Peter is not so keen. However, she hopes that once they get married, Peter will change his mind. Jenny feels that men are often slower to accept the responsibilities and commitment of parenthood. So, she decides to wait until she thinks the time is right before she broaches the subject with Peter.

Peter, on the other hand, is not aware of Jenny's desire to have children. The only time they discussed the issue, he made his feelings clear. As far as he can recall, Jenny agreed – at least she certainly did not disagree. That was a few years ago. The topic has not come up since, so Peter is quite certain that they think alike.

Their wedding day is wonderful – it is all that Jenny had hoped it would be. However, they are hardly back from their honeymoon when Jenny brings up the subject of having a baby. She had planned to wait for a year or so before doing this, but suddenly she feels a strong urge to share her thoughts and dreams with Peter now that they are a married couple.

Peter's reaction is a complex mixture of negative emotions:

- **Shock** – where has this sudden impulse come from?

- **Disbelief** – when they last discussed the issue, Jenny had not said she wanted children

- **Feeling trapped** – how can Jenny say this now – why not before they got married?

- **Resentment** – they are just back from honeymoon, and Peter is feeling closer to Jenny than ever before

- **Anger** – if having children is so important to Jenny, Peter sees that he is in a lose-lose situation. Either he agrees against his will or he becomes the villain of the peace.

No wonder that Peter feels as he does. Why did Jenny not express her hopes and expectations to him before now? Jenny tells him that she did not want to spoil the happiness they were enjoying by introducing a topic that might upset Peter. When she heard him say he did not want children, she was concerned. But she thought that his thinking would change once they were married.

Was Jenny afraid that Peter would call off the wedding if he realised that she wanted children?
How does she expect him to react now?
Where do they go from here?

REFLECTION

The moral of this story is clear – talk to your partner about the issues that are important to you BEFORE the wedding. Getting married does not change you or your partner. You will both be the same people afterwards – hopefully happier, of course, but your firmly held beliefs and convictions are not going to change substantially after a wedding ceremony.

LAYING DOWN GOOD FOUNDATIONS

We are all creatures of habit. As you have been getting to know one another, without necessarily realising it, you and your partner have established behaviour patterns.

It is good to recognise the **positive behaviour patterns** you have already developed in your relationship.

1. *We like to go out together on Friday nights – usually to one of our favourite restaurants.*

If there is one ingredient guaranteed to keep the magic in your lives, it is **Date Night**. Once a couple commits to going out together on a regular basis, the chances are that they will continue to communicate effectively. For no matter what stresses or challenges arise during the week, they can look forward to that oasis of calm and relaxation, where each will feel heard by the other.

It is important to note that Date Night is not the same as going out with friends. That, of course, is also fun and necessary. But setting aside quality time for just the two of you means that you can continue to grow in knowledge of one another, deepen your connection and keep the spark of romance alive.

2. *I like it when we make time to chat before going to bed.*

Making time to talk to one another is a most effective way of reconnecting at the end of each day. Think of it as part of what I call **The Three T's**:

Talking

Touching

Time together.

No matter how close you feel to one another, by the end of a busy day without contact, a reconnection is needed. It is all a question of communication. If your partner does not know what your day has been like, it is difficult to imagine how you are feeling.

3. *My fiancé(e) is so responsive – everything I do for him/her is appreciated.*

Being **appreciative** of one another is wonderful. You are no doubt excited at this pre-marriage stage, so it is natural that you find it easy to express your positive feelings to each other. The challenge, once again, is to keep that awareness alive, not to take your partner's good qualities for granted later on; to continue to be mindful of his/her love, respect and trust.

A Note of Warning

Be careful that certain behaviour patterns do not induce **unrealistic expectations**

- He always texts me at work before I text him.

- We understand each other completely. I don't need to tell her what I think – she knows instinctively.

Such assumptions can make us blind to the changing dynamic in a relationship. So, when he doesn't text her, she is determined not to text him; or when he feels misunderstood, he is shocked – does that mean she doesn't care about him anymore?

How are you going to ensure that the positive behaviour patterns you have now remain part of your lives when you are married? Talk to each other – make a few commitments. And remember, no stand offs in the future:

It's his/her turn now, so I'm just going to wait and see.

If nothing happens, then it's his/her fault.

You are both on the same team from now on, so be a team player.

REFLECTION
the **WITT** technique.

I devised this simple mnemonic to help couples check that they are communicating effectively. Try to incorporate this four-letter acronym into your communication toolkit. It is particularly useful when you feel upset or annoyed with your partner.

W – Wording – choose the right words to express what you feel. AVOID:

- Accusations or overly emotional language – *How dare you…*

- Exaggerated language – *I have never been so insulted in all my life.*

- Generalisations – *You always…* or *You never…*

Opt instead for something like:

- *I felt really hurt when you…*

  OR

- *I was surprised by your behaviour last night. It was not like you to behave in that way.*

I – Incident – keep to the issue at hand. Talk about the particular incident, and your feelings around it. Avoid bringing up other incidents from the past. This only confuses the argument. It also opens up the floor to both of you to bring up any residual hurts from the past. Once a pile of grievances has built up, chances are that nothing will be resolved.

T – Timing – Choose a time to address the issue when you are both calm. If you are feeling angry, take time out to calm yourself down first. This will mean that you can put the issue into perspective and be better able to express your feelings rationally.

T – Tone – this simple word is dynamite in a relationship. Try saying, *Oh, I see*, using different tones. You can sound sarcastic, disbelieving, angry or sincere. Amazing, isn't it?

Now think of the tone in which you like to be addressed. Can you use this tone when discussing the issue with your partner?

CONCLUSION

Achieving and maintaining effective communication is a constant challenge, even when couples feel close and in love. The more aware you are of any poor communication habits, the more you can strive to address them and give clear, balanced, and respectful messages to your partner.

To feel that you each understand one another, that you are on the same team, is truly magical.

Chapter 6
All About Feelings

The word *feeling* has a broad application – ranging from a physical sensation to a psychological or emotional response or awareness. In this chapter, we are talking about emotion. But our emotions can also have a physical dimension. Do you consider yourself good at recognising and naming your emotions?

Feelings come and go. We are not always in control of our emotions. And sometimes, it is difficult to find the words to express how we feel. Yet, it is how we react to our feelings that really matters. Do you find it easy to tell your partner how you are really feeling?

Ever hear yourself snap – *What do you mean, I'm sounding angry?*

Recognising and articulating feelings can be a challenge. Let's look at your childhood and see what messages you received about expressing emotions back then.

FEELINGS QUIZ – CHILDHOOD MESSAGES

- Were you and your siblings encouraged to talk about your feelings?

- To whom did you express your feelings as a child?

- When your parents got angry, how was it expressed?
- When you were a child, where did you feel safest?
- Do you think you felt generally happy or unhappy growing up?
- When you expressed your feelings as a child, what was the reaction?

FEELINGS – THE WORDS TO SAY THEM

How are you doing?
Ok, thanks. And you?
Fine. Yeah, I'm fine.

It is impossible to know what either person is feeling here because neither of them has named an emotion. There are many ways of communicating feelings, other than verbally – tone of voice, body language, eye contact or lack of it. But often the person who has difficulty in naming and communicating feelings can also use camouflage. The tone remains pleasant but forced.

We all hide our true emotions at times. You are hardly going to share your innermost feelings with anyone who asks. But, with your partner it needs to be different. Your partner deserves and wants to know how you are feeling inside. Words like *ok* and *fine* say nothing about what is really going on in your head.

Expressing emotions openly is very culturally dependent. In some cultures, the open expression of feelings is quite acceptable, and indeed, expected. In others, it is neither expected nor accepted. As you grow and develop, your environment dictates what behaviour is acceptable. From a young age, you are taught how to respond to and express emotion.

There can also be a gender bias regarding the expression of emotion. *Big boys don't cry* has had a hugely repressive effect on generations of men in many cultures. The message here is clear. Boys must learn to repress, rather than express their feelings. The subtext is that the expression of emotions other than anger, is considered non-masculine. In this cultural context, only girls are allowed to cry. And crying can be used to express so many emotions – sadness, joy, anger, frustration, loneliness, rejection, fear. The list goes on.

It is really not surprising, then, that many people, especially men who have been brought up in an emotionally repressive environment, have difficulty in recognising and expressing their feelings, even with their life partners. The thinking and behaviour from childhood must be unravelled before they can become comfortable with their emotions.

You, like all humans, have an emotional side, a part of the self that reacts instinctively and sensitively to each experience. This aspect of your nature must be given expression if you are to develop as a complete human being. Because, it is through emotion that we make sense of our experience.

The first challenge is to be able to recognise and name your own feelings. The next challenge is to communicate those feelings to your partner.

FEELING EXERCISE

This exercise can be fun as well as challenging. You and your partner can do this any time you are alone together – in the car, out for a walk, at home. Just follow the steps below:

First, you name a feeling – happiness, sadness, joy, anxiety, hope, resentment...
Then your partner has to:

1. Define the feeling word, saying what it means to him/her.

2. Next, describe the physical impact of the feeling – laughter, tension, rapid heartbeat...

3. Finally, describe an incident, recent or from the past, when they experienced that feeling.

4. Now the roles are reversed – so it's your turn.

5. The more you can practise this simple exercise, the more familiar you will become with recognising your own feelings and those of your partner.

Next comes a reflective exercise where you look at a past experience in greater depth.

REFLECTION ONE

Think of an incident from your past that upset you. This can be something that happened when you were a child or a recent event.

1. Briefly describe the incident.

2. Are you able to recall how you reacted when it first occurred?

3. What did you do?

4. What were your feelings at the time?

5. How did you deal with those feelings – did you express them, repress them, confide in someone?

6. Now that you are back there in that time, are you aware of feeling any of these emotions again?

7. Can you name them? How about anger, hurt, sadness, frustration, anxiety, self-pity, disgust, humiliation?

8. Can you recall any physical sensations associated with the incident?

9. Are you happy with how the incident was dealt with?

10. If not, what would you have liked to see happen?

11. Share your story with your partner. If your partner has not already done so, ask him/her to tell you about an incident in their past which caused anxiety or hurt. Try to encourage your partner to name the emotions felt at the time.

REFLECTION TWO

Having completed Reflection One, you are now hopefully more conscious of your own emotions. The next challenge is to become aware of your partner's feelings.

Consider the following questions either together or separately:

1. Do you think you are good at reading your partner's feelings?

2. What key signs of stress, anxiety, anger, hurt can you recognise in your partner?

3. How do you react when your partner seems stressed? Do you tend to ignore the negative emotions or address them?

4. If you address the issue, how does your partner usually respond?

5. Is it easy or difficult for you to express your feelings?

6. Do you help each other to feel comfortable about acknowledging feelings?

7. How does each of you express anger?

8. Could each of you handle anger better? If so, how?

9. What about positive feelings – love, joy, admiration? How do you both express these?

10. Do you think you could convey positive feelings to each other more often?

11. When was the last time you told your partner:
I really admire you for…?

If you have answered separately, share your responses with your partner. Take your time with each question. Do you feel more comfortable talking about your feelings now? If yes, well done. If not, keep talking. Focus on your feelings until you can recognise and name them. Does your partner now find it any easier?

If you still find it difficult to access your own feelings, see *Difficulty Recognising Feelings* – No. 6 in the Troubleshooting Guide (p. 115).

EMOTIONAL FLOODING

Have you ever become overpowered by a strong rush of emotion? This experience is known as emotional flooding. We can sometimes feel so overwhelmed that we cannot think clearly. The logical left side of the brain has been taken over by the emotional right side, so it is hard to proceed rationally. If you ever feel overwhelmed by your feelings, it is good to have a strategy in place.

Take a few breaths, then try to focus on what you are actually doing at this moment – writing, walking, having a cup of tea. As you allow your actions become reality, the mind calms down.

Try to remember the golden rule – wait until you have calmed yourself down, until you no longer feel overwhelmed by emotion, before you engage in dialogue. By then you should be able to think and respond to the situation in a rational way.

PERPETUATING POSITIVITY

At this exciting time of your life, you are no doubt experiencing lots of happy feelings. So, this is a good time to resolve to keep positivity in your lives together into the future. There are very many ways to achieve this – simple things like smiling, listening attentively, offering to help others, and being generous with your praise.

There is no denying that it is good for us all to receive praise. No matter how much you may protest that it is undeserved or unnecessary, receiving praise generates a little inner glow which makes us feel happier.

Many couples are appreciative of what their partners do and thank them from time to time. But it is also good to compliment them on what they have done well or tell them how great they are. Praise given readily and regularly goes a long way to helping couples feel happy and close.

CONCLUSION

Remember that we are not always in charge of our feelings – they come and go. But, by recognising and processing them, we can deal with them in a safe and healthy way. If you are aware of an underlying sense that you would like to feel happier, see *Dealing with a Niggling Sense of Unhappiness* – No. 7 in the Troubleshooting Guide (p. 116).

Being aware of your own feelings will also help you recognise how your partner feels. Once you know that you are on the same wavelength, your joy is doubled.

Chapter 7
Dealing with Conflict

The juxtaposition of opposites, of positive and negative, generates energy and life.

If we were all the same, all agreeing on every issue, life would be dull indeed.

There would be no variety, no disagreements, no challenges.

Conflict happens. This is neither wrong nor bad. Whenever two people get together, there is the potential for opposing needs or opinions. Even when these two people are in a loving relationship, planning to marry and spend the rest of their lives together, the possibility of conflict is still there. For no two people think exactly alike all the time – at least not if each of them feels free to express their own opinion.

There is nothing surprising or wrong about clashing opinions or attitudes. What is important is how each of you reacts when confrontation happens. Are you inclined to become angry, defensive, really offended? Do you tend to interpret a difference of opinion as a personal insult?

How do you react when your partner has upset you? Can you see some of yourself in one of the roles below?

Escalator – when you sense conflict in the air, the heat is turned up; verbal attack is met by counterattack; past incidents are churned up and thrown at one another. Each wants to be heard, yet neither of you is listening to the other.

Withdrawer – once you hear your partner's voice escalate, you retreat into your corner, back to the safety of silence. No matter what is said, you refuse to be goaded. You feel somewhat smug, yet safe in your silence. But you also feel a bit worthless at times – *Nothing I do is ever good enough*.

Pursuer – you are constantly dissatisfied with how your partner reacts to you. You want more attention. The more he/she resorts to silence, the more frustrated you become. Yes, you shout and even scream at times, *just to get him/her to listen*. But the louder you shout, the less chance you have of being heard.

What do you notice about those three roles? There is not much **mutual respect** being shown, is there? In each instance, whoever is speaking wants to be heard, but the higher the **volume** knob is turned up, the less effective the communication. The Withdrawer totally refuses to engage and resorts to silence.

There is also not much real **listening** going on here.

What **tone** of voice do you imagine is used in each of the three scenarios outlined above?

As you prepare for your marriage, it is a really good time to agree on some Ground Rules for Confrontation. You may find the suggestions below helpful.

BITING THE BULLET – GROUND RULES FOR CONFRONTATION

1. **Mutual respect.** Calm down. You are probably feeling angry with your partner right now. But try not to allow your anger make you disrespectful. Your partner has feelings and needs too.

2. **No shouting.** Conflict can only be resolved if you can talk to one another as calmly as possible.

3. **No name calling.** Name calling is never acceptable, no matter how angry you feel. Walk away until you have calmed down. Then return and address the issue.

4. **Avoid 'You' statements.** When we feel angry with someone, it is easy but dangerous to start a conversation with accusations.

    a. *You're such a…*

    b. *You don't care about me.*

    c. *What do you mean… What about your behaviour?*

   Once your partner hears these accusations, he/she will most likely go into defensive mode. In other words, instead of listening to you, your partner will start preparing a defence or a counterattack.

5. **Use 'I' statements** – *I feel angry, annoyed, hurt…*
   By telling your partner how you feel, you paint the picture from your perspective. Describe your emotions. Go deeper than your anger. Underneath anger there are usually other feelings – loneliness, sadness, isolation, resentment, or feelings of neglect

or alienation. Stop and identify the core emotion you are feeling.

6. **Echoes from the past.** When you feel angry and upset, ask yourself, *when did I last feel like this?* Follow the lead back along the chain of memories. Can you recall feeling like this as a child? What were the circumstances? What were your fears back then – fear of disapproval, abandonment, failure? Perhaps the key to your present reaction is right here. Share your memories with your partner.

7. **No pileups.** Confine your argument with your partner to the present situation. This means that you discuss only the incident to hand. Avoid dredging up all the other times that you have become annoyed with your partner. Your argument weakens as one offence is piled on another. It carries more weight and conviction if it is precise.

8. **Avoid generalisations.** *You always...* or, *You never...*
Once your partner hears these general statements, the tendency is to switch off – here we go again, same old, same old... You have both been down this well-worn path before and it only goes around in circles.

9. **Take turns** in presenting your case. No matter how strongly you feel about your situation, you must respect your partner's right of reply. You should allow one another equal time to speak without interruption.

Watch out for being dismissive of what your partner is saying. This negative attitude can be communicated verbally or by your body language – the shrug, the rolling eyes, the sighs. Where is mutual respect here?

10. **Listen carefully** to your partner. When you are feeling angry or annoyed, it is very easy to focus solely on what you want to say. Even as your partner is speaking, you may find yourself preparing your counterargument.

    This is counterproductive. It means that you are not prepared to consider looking at the situation from another perspective. Therefore, it is unlikely that you will reach a resolution.

11. **Give feedback**. There is nothing better for diffusing an argument, than for each side to feel that they have been really heard. To show your partner that you have truly listened, try giving a synopsis of what has been said.

    Start with – *What I have heard you say is...* As you give this feedback, avoid inputting your own viewpoint, commentary, or self-defence. The objective here is to tell your partner that you have got his/her message, even if you don't agree with it.

12. **Establish your own ground rules**. Now that you have considered the above suggestions, it is time for you both to negotiate your own ground rules. Perhaps you would like to rule out some negative attitude or behaviour which occurs whenever you have a confrontation.

13. **Agree to differ**. It is perfectly natural that no two people agree on absolutely everything. The disagreement itself need not have a negative effect on your relationship; it is how you both handle a disagreement that matters. For further ideas, see *When Couples Differ* – No. 1 in the Troubleshooting Guide (p. 108).

FINDING A RESOLUTION

When both of you have spoken and each feels heard, it is time to ask what you want to see happening. Perhaps, having listened carefully to your partner's view, you will each decide to make a small change in attitude. Or maybe now that you are more aware of how your partner feels, you can resolve to make a behavioural change.

One of the simplest ways of reaching a resolution is the **twin-track approach**.

Each of you first volunteers to make a change:

e.g. *I will try to listen more fully and not to go into defensive mode whenever I feel that you are upset with me.*

You then each outline the change you most want to see in your partner:

e.g. *When you are upset, I would like you to speak in a calmer tone. Once you raise your voice, I feel frightened and get too upset to listen to you.*

Ideally, you can each accept the change requested by your partner.

CONFRONTATION REVIEW

Once sufficient time has elapsed, after negotiating a resolution to confrontation, it is good to look back and see if there are any lessons to be learned which will help you next time.

Below is a reminder of the WITT checklist, which may be helpful in reviewing the situation.

1. **W**ording – can you recall any phrases or words that were particularly hurtful or difficult for you? Was the language you used to your partner overly emotive?

2. **I**ncident – did you both manage to stick to the matter in hand? Did either of you fall into the generalisation trap?

3. **T**one – were you aware of the tone of voice you used? Did you both respect one another – avoiding sarcasm, anger and raised voices?

4. **T**iming – when and how did the confrontation start? Were there signs of mounting tension that you could have addressed at an earlier stage?

If you are unhappy with the way you handled the last confrontation, think about it, and then talk to you partner. Be prepared to acknowledge your role in letting things escalate or go off track. Once you recognise where things can improve, you are well on the way to a more effective pattern of handling conflict in the future.

This technique of handling confrontation in an effective way has a much wider application. Once you have mastered it, you will be able to use it to great effect in any situation where conflict occurs.

If confrontation is a recurring theme in your relationship, see *Constant Conflict* – No. 8 in the Troubleshooting Guide (p. 119).

DEALING WITH STRESS

Did you ever experience confrontation and later realise that you were quite stressed beforehand? Here are two strategies that I have found very effective.

1. CALMING EXERCISE

When things get too hectic, it is good to take time out to follow a simple routine. This is a handy way to bring about some inner peace. Try to make it part of your daily routine.

Time required – TWO minutes.

What to do:

- Find a quiet space away from everyone.

- Put your phone on silent.

- Sit down and make yourself comfortable.

- Rest both feet on the floor and place your hands on the arms of the chair.

- Close your eyes and focus on your breathing. Think: *I breathe in peace and calm; I breathe out stress and tension.*

- Starting with your head, think RELAX and SLOWLY, progressing right down to your toes.

- Focus on Touch – your back against the back of the chair, your arms, your hands, your legs, your feet.

- Next, focus on the Sounds around you – just let them come and go.

- Focus on Smell – can you identify any?

- Focus on Taste – are you aware of any taste in your mouth?

- Remind yourself – *I breathe in peace and calm; I breathe out stress and tension.*

- Sight. Slowly, open your eyes and focus on your surroundings – what do you see?

- Now, focus again on your breathing – is it more relaxed? Are you more relaxed?

If so, well done. Now that you have completed this short exercise, see if you have managed to put your myriad tasks and pressures into perspective.

If you still feel under pressure, try the technique outlined below.

2. PRIORITISING TASKS

This is a really useful strategy – by the time you have put the issue into perspective, you will already feel more in control.

Consider which category best fits the matter in hand:

- Vital and urgent – if so, do it yourself right now. If not, can you delegate this to someone else?

- Important but not urgent – in this case, postpone and plan it in your timeline.

- Unimportant and not urgent – drop it and forget it.

Do you feel better now?

Once you have de-stressed yourself, you will probably find that you are in a better frame of mind. You can now put any disagreements with your partner into perspective.

However, if you have difficulty in reaching a resolution to a disagreement, see *When We Still Disagree – What Next?* – No. 9 in the Troubleshooting Guide (p. 120).

CONCLUSION

Confrontation happens – but don't confuse it with competition. There should be no winners or losers here. You are both on the same team – remember? By truly listening and being respectful to one another, you will be able to view your differences as opportunities for your relationship to grow and deepen.

Remember – love is not expressed by negative behaviour.

Chapter 8
Revealing the Hidden You

My work in counselling clients over three decades has convinced me that mutual respect and trust create the best conditions for a loving relationship to develop and thrive. I hope that, by now, you too recognise this. Just think of the people in your life who have earned your respect. What aspects of their personality do you most admire?

And, what about trust? What causes you to trust another person? When you feel comfortable around someone, do you feel that they would honour confidentiality if you were to share a secret with them?

Now that you have found a life partner, can you envisage sharing your inner thoughts with him/her? Do you feel that your secrets will be safe; that your vulnerability will be respected? If so, that is a positive reflection of your relationship.

SECRETS AND LIES

Is there anything you cannot discuss with your partner? Are there some events in your past that you have not shared with him/her? If so, stop and think about it now.

Ask yourself – *What is the worst thing that could happen if I spoke to my partner about this?*

Let's consider some of the responses that clients have given me over the years.

1. ***Our relationship might fall apart.***

    On what basis might you make this assumption? If there is something in your past life that you would rather not share with your partner, what does that say about the relationship?

    When, as will most likely happen, your partner finally discovers the truth, how will he/she feel?

- Confused – *why did you not tell me before now? Don't you trust me?*

- Disappointed – *I thought that we had an open relationship, that we kept no secrets from each other.*

- Angry – *how could you try to deceive me, hoping that I'd never find out?*

- Resentment – *is that the only thing you have not shared with me, or are there other secrets?*

2. ***My partner would be disappointed in me.***

    Not half as disappointed as he/she will be to discover the truth later on.

    Now is the time to share – a relationship built on trust is a strong relationship.

3. ***I can't find the words to say it.***

    Just try. Choose a time when you are alone together and free from distraction. Approach the subject gently. If you feel uncomfortable, tell your partner. A loving partner will be supportive and caring. This is a good opportunity to see how the two of you will handle difficult situations in the future.

4. *I am too embarrassed to talk about this to my partner.*

What is marriage all about? Is it about keeping up appearances or about sharing your lives in the most intimate way possible?

When you first started dating, were you very fussy about your appearance? By now, no doubt while you still like to look smart, you feel more relaxed in each other's company. That is part of the joy brought about by increased physical intimacy.

So, too, with emotional intimacy. Holding on to your secrets means that there is a part of yourself that you are not prepared to share. If your partner loves you, he/she will want to know the full you – not just a version of yourself that you choose to present. That is not being honest.

No matter how hard it is to share your secret with your partner, it will be a great relief to know that you are no longer carrying this burden on your own. So, go for it.

You owe it to yourself and to your partner.

If the idea of sharing fully with your partner is too great a challenge, see *Dealing with Residual Fears* – No. 10 in the Troubleshooting Guide (p. 122).

SHARING MAY BE CARING BUT IT CAN ALSO BE SCARY

If you have something that you consider to be a deep fear or dark secret, it is important that you can talk to your partner about it. This requires great trust on your part and respect and confidentiality from your partner. But once you have taken this leap of faith, you will no doubt feel closer than ever before.

SHARING EXERCISE

Tell your partner that you want to share something difficult with him/her.

- Set time apart for this – a downtime for you both, without outside interference.

- Tell your partner how you are feeling – nervous, anxious, hopeful.

- Then share your fear or secret.

- Talk slowly so your partner can understand more fully.

- When you have finished, pause, and wait.

- Give your partner time to ask any questions to clarify your story.

- If you feel upset, allow yourself to be comforted – even big boys can and should cry sometimes.

- See how your partner is feeling – shocked, saddened, angry for your sake, relieved?

- Talk about what you want to see happening now – is the problem halved now that it is shared, or do you want to take some action?

- Thank your partner for listening to you – this is what a good relationship is all about.

Sharing your secret fears with one another can help build your emotional connection. You now have found someone whom you can trust – someone in whom you can confide your greatest secrets. And you, in turn, will treasure and respect your partner's secrets or fears.

Risk reaching out to one another. This is what marriage is all about – **risking, reaching out, respecting one another.** For by sharing yourselves intimately, both emotionally and physically, you create a unique and special bond, which will grow stronger with time.

If you still find it too difficult to be fully open with your partner, see *When a Secret Is Too Big* – No. 11 in the Troubleshooting Guide (p. 123).

CONCLUSION

If you already enjoy an open and frank relationship with your partner, you have probably skipped through this chapter. If there are a few no-go areas between you, I hope that the exercises outlined here have helped. Remember that honesty with one another is certainly the best policy. It will allow your relationship develop and thrive.

Chapter 9
Let's Talk About Sex

We are sexual beings. Our sexual appetite is as natural as our appetite for food or our need for shelter. It is an integral part of us as humans. This sexual appetite finds its most fulfilling expression in a loving relationship. In fact, it is an essential and integral part of married life. Just think about it – if the sexual and intimate parts of your relationship are removed, you may as well be brother and sister or simply friends, sharing accommodation.

Some couples decide to defer having a fully sexual relationship until they are married. They enjoy exploring the pleasures of being intimate together without sexual intercourse. Other couples are happy to start a full sexual relationship at an earlier stage. Either way, it is important that everyone preparing for marriage is informed about sex and feels comfortable with their sexuality.

SEXUAL ATTRACTION

Do you realise that the attraction you felt for one another from the start of your relationship was primarily sexually driven? Our brains respond to the visual in a sensual way, which, in turn, connects to sexual arousal. We all have, at a subconscious if not conscious level, an inbuilt desire to choose a partner with whom we feel sexually compatible.

If you want to have children, you are also programmed, at a subconscious level, to choose a partner whom you consider suitable as a parent for your future children. Humans, like other creatures, look for behavioural tendencies, physical features and personality traits that enhance our chances of survival and procreation.

Women need protection during pregnancy, and therefore seek a partner with whom they feel safe. Men are most attracted to women during their fertile years, thus enhancing the chances of procreation.

Humans have an inbuilt desire and need for connection with another human being. Making love is a way by which this innate need is met. Lovemaking binds us together in a special emotional bond.

Unlike casual sexual encounters, the sexual relationship between a committed couple is a work in progress – a journey of intimacy, trust and friendship that deepens as your life together unfolds. And this journey is unique to every couple.

The beauty and dignity of sexual love finds its true expression in marriage. Now each of you can relax and be your true selves, secure in the knowledge that this most intimate of acts is just for the two of you. You can be vulnerable together, sharing your bare selves with one another.

As your sexual journey progresses, you will find that making love takes on a new meaning – it becomes more truly an expression of deepening love and connection, allowing you to express your deepest self in a most intimate and sharing way

Sex is also fun. If that is not the case for you, think about it. Can you introduce an element of lightness or fun into your sex life? What would you like to experience – what would your partner like?

THE MANY LANGUAGES OF SEXUAL LOVE

Read the list below and see if you can identify these elements in your intimacy and lovemaking.

GENTLENESS – Making love is about being tender and caring together in this most intimate and bonding experience.

RESPECT – By respecting the dignity and individuality of the other, each is allowed to feel safe, secure, and valued. This, in turn, helps you both become your best selves.

TRUST – Being able to trust allows you both to feel secure enough to relax and become vulnerable as you share your intimate selves with one another.

GIVING and RECEIVING – In lovemaking, you can give and receive both pleasure and affirmation. Thinking about pleasuring the other in the act of love affirms your sense of self and other.

CONNECTION – Feeling the great joy of connection with another at this deep level is the fulfilment of a primal desire in us all.

COMMUNICATION – Speaking about lovemaking helps you become aware of your partner's needs. By listening to one another, you ensure that you are always there for one another.

APPRECIATION – It is good to try always to be appreciative of the great privilege of the sexual act itself; to appreciate the wonder of the possibility of new life, of having a family of your own.

ROLES IN MAKING AND EXPRESSING LOVE

A sexual relationship works best when each partner is happy to initiate both sexual intimacy and affection. By showing affection in many little ways, you keep in touch with one another. A few loving words, an unexpected hug, a note left under the pillow, a surprise kiss… Such little gestures can make a big impact. Your partner feels loved and cherished. There is then a natural progression to expressing your love in a sexual way.

What role do you play in your sexual relationship?

- Are you the one who suggests sex almost all of the time? This can leave little room for your partner to initiate. What would it be like if your partner initiated sometimes? Wouldn't it be good to be on the receiving end of desire?

- Maybe you are more the love bunny, always wanting to cuddle, but not so interested in having sex? What message do you want to give your partner – *I love being with you, but don't ask me to have sex every time I touch you. Can't we sometimes be affectionate without it always having to lead to full intercourse?* Talk about this together.

- Or are you reluctant to initiate sex or affection? Do you feel too uncomfortable? Are you afraid of being rejected? If so, ask yourself the question – *What is the worst thing that can happen if I initiate sex?* Is it that your partner will say no? That may indeed happen. But can you live with that? Think about it.

- If you have a tendency to dominate, it might be good to try breaking this pattern of behaviour. The excitement of being desired, the joy of showing affection, the challenge of risking rejection – these are all worthwhile experiences.

TALKING ABOUT SEX

As with every other aspect of your relationship, **communication** is the key to success. It is not reasonable to expect your partner to know how you feel about sex if you don't articulate your thoughts and feelings. If you feel uncomfortable about bringing up the topic of sex with your partner, try reading the following statements together.

- *A man falls in love because of the way he feels when he is with a woman. He needs sexual fulfilment in order to respond emotionally. To a man, sex is a most meaningful way of expressing emotion. It makes him feel fulfilled, more of a man.*

- *A woman needs emotional fulfilment before she responds sexually. She needs to feel loved and appreciated, that her man cares about her, before she is interested in engaging in sex.*

How does each of you react to these statements? They are certainly generalisations – but are they somewhat true for you? The more you can articulate your feelings around sex, the more insight your partner gains. Listen carefully and patiently as your partner speaks.

REFLECTION

Consider the following questions. They start by looking at the messages you received about sex in childhood. Ask your partner to do the same.

It may help you to jot down your responses.

- When and from whom did you first learn about sex?

- Was sex talked about openly at home or was it never mentioned?

- What about the language used when talking about sex? Was it:

    - obscure and inaccessible
    - vulgar and profane
    - balanced and respectful?

- What was the main message about sex that you received from your parents?

- When you hear the word SEX now, what is your immediate reaction – embarrassment, excitement, anxiety, curiosity?

- Are you happy with your attitude to sex today or do you find it rather childish? If you are uncomfortable, try saying the word aloud a few times. There is no great mystique to it, really.

- Think again about the word SEX – what thoughts or sensations spring to mind? Can you name some of your feelings? Is your attitude to sex overall positive or negative?

- On a list of priorities in the relationship with your partner, where do you rank sexuality and intimacy – high, medium, or low?

- Consider your sex life with your partner. Allow yourself three wishes – first, a long term one. If you could add one ingredient to sex with your partner on an ongoing basis, what would it be?

- Next, if you were to tell your partner how you would like to be pleasured during lovemaking, what would you say?

- Now for the third wish. If you could choose any setting for romantic, passionate, fulfilling sex with your partner, what would it be? Don't be modest here – forget about practicalities and costs – the sky's the limit.

- So, what did you come up with in that third wish? Which elements of the scenario appeal to you most? Could you replicate some or all of this scenario here and now? How about it? How do you think your partner will react? Find out.

COMMON MYTHS ABOUT SEX

What are your fundamental beliefs about sex? Remember that we are all products of our familial and cultural backgrounds. It is good to examine some common myths and see what messages we have consciously or subconsciously absorbed.

1. **Real men are always ready for sex.** What are the implications of this statement? Is it that only men who are fixated with sex qualify as masculine and macho? Think of the pressure this puts on men, especially during adolescence.

2. **Good girls don't express sexual desires.** What or who is a 'good girl'? There is a clearly defined division here between the girls who are fun to be with, and the good but serious girls, who are not allowed to express sexual feelings. In many ways, this reflects the polarity that exists in the representation of sex in different cultures, where sex is considered either vulgar and profane, or sinful and embarrassing.

3. **If you don't use it, you lose it.** This myth is responsible for much of the poor lovemaking experienced by couples today. It usually starts in adolescence when boys first discover masturbation. There is a sense of urgency, a rush to climax before they are discovered.

   But the truth is, a man can have an erection, lose it, and get another, any number of times, before climaxing. This realisation allows lovemaking to be prolonged and more meaningful to both parties.

4. **A woman's role is to satisfy a man.** Hopefully, this is not too widely accepted by either men or women today. Yet, some women still resign themselves to the role of constant giver, while ignoring their own sexual needs. Over time, then, lovemaking loses its excitement for both parties. The man feels less comfortable at imposing himself on a somewhat passive spouse, while she becomes increasingly detached and disinterested.

5. **All lovemaking should end in intercourse.** It has to be said that men are usually guilty here. The male sexual drive is such that once aroused, a man wants to proceed to climax. His partner, on the other hand, may seek intimacy and comfort, without wanting full sexual intercourse. A lack of understanding here can lead to an impasse and cause tension. Talk about it.

6. **Sex should always be spontaneous.** There is, of course, something magical when mutual arousal leads to spontaneous sex. But let's admit it, life happens. We can get so caught up in the everyday business of life, that there is no time left for sexual intimacy. This is where it is good to realise that we schedule into our day the things we consider important – meals, meetings, work. Why not make time for sex?

7. **If my partner loves me, he/she should know how I feel.** Some couples are quite comfortable to talk about sex. For others, it can be a real challenge. Women are usually good at communicating their feelings. Yet, when it comes to sex, they sometimes shy away from articulating their needs and desires. This can stem from childhood messages where sex was not discussed, or from some subconscious idea that sex is vulgar or sinful.

WHEN TALKING ABOUT SEX SEEMS TOO DIFFICULT

For some couples, the idea of having a frank discussion about sex is really daunting. There may be a fear of upsetting a partner; a fear of seeming too demanding; indeed, quite a deep level of discomfort around the whole topic.

Our sexual needs, patterns and desires are so intimate and personal that we can become overly sensitive and defensive. But establishing a few Ground Rules can create a situation where couples feel more comfortable. See what you think about the suggested list below and then establish your own.

GROUND RULES

- Choose a **good time** to talk about your sex life – when you both feel relaxed and comfortable. Say, *I'd like us to talk about our sex life. Is now a good time for you?*

- **Respect** each other's thoughts or desires. Try a listening exercise to start – one of you speaks about your sex life. The other partner listens and then gives feedback on what has been said. Remember, in feedback, avoid giving your reaction – just report what you have heard. There will be time later for you to express your thoughts on the subject.

- Agree to keep your discussion **confidential**. This is really important. It will make each of you feel more comfortable talking about sex.

- Have you some **secret desires** regarding sex which you have never articulated? Now is the time to share them with your partner. Forget the shyness – after all, what have you got to lose?

- Be as **open minded** as you can to what your partner is saying. If you feel shocked or disgusted, tell your partner that you are uncomfortable. Then explore your reaction a bit more. Ask your partner to explain themselves more fully.

- Agree to respect each other's **boundaries**. A loving partner will not wish to do or say anything which the other finds offensive. But sometimes, it is good to open your mind before you close it.

- If one partner has **little or no interest** in sex, this usually indicates that the lovemaking pattern being used is not meeting their needs. In other words, he/she is not getting sufficient pleasure from lovemaking. In that case, ask your partner to teach you how to improve as a lover.

- If either of you feels that there is a real **sexual dysfunction**, agree to seek professional help. For a man, the problem may be related to difficulty achieving or maintaining an erection. For a woman, it could be painful intercourse. But, remember that sometimes a couple can resolve these issues themselves simply by being very attentive to what each partner is saying. Once each of you feels heard, it can make lovemaking more relaxed. That can go a long way to resolving a sexual problem.

- **Don't forget, making love should be fun.** So be prepared to laugh when things go wrong. It is not the end of the world. Try not to be too serious or earnest about sex. Remember that you have a whole lifetime ahead of you to get it right.

- If you still need convincing about the importance of intimacy in your relationship, check out *What Makes Intimacy So Special* – No. 12 in the Troubleshooting Guide (p. 124).

CONCLUSION

Several studies indicate that married people have **more frequent and more enjoyable sex** than singles. This is not surprising. After all, when you are in a committed relationship you have more time to focus on deepening your connection. There is no longer any need to spend time looking for a sexual partner. Hence, married people can develop a better feel for and awareness of each other's sexual and intimacy needs.

You may also be interested to note some of the psychological and physical benefits of a happy consensual sexual relationship. Having sex with a loving partner:

- Boosts self-esteem

- Reduces stress levels

- Releases endorphins for happiness and oxytocin for calmness

- Keeps you fit
- Improves cognitive functioning

- Improves your general health

The sexual journey with your partner is ongoing. Make it a voyage of discovery, change and mutual pleasure.

Chapter 10
Being Part of a Team Without Losing Your Identity

DO WE MAKE A GOOD TEAM?

We are all connected to one another as humans. We are all connected to our environment, all part of the universe.

So, when we feel disconnected, it alarms and upsets us. This is especially true if we feel estranged from the person we love best.

Un Homme et Une Femme

Ever hear of this classic French movie? So much of art and literature attempts to understand the essential differences between the sexes. It is risky to make generalisations, but there are certain traits that are more common to one gender than another. So here goes.

A Man

- falls in love with a woman because he feels good when he is with her.

- tends to cover up his negative emotions, especially those of hurt or inadequacy.

- may think that expressing feelings of sadness, hurt or rejection makes him less of a man – big boys don't cry.

- focuses more on the physical, reacting to what he sees and perceives, rather than picking up on emotional cues.

- can seem thoughtless at times – unaware of a woman's expectations or needs.

- sometimes needs to be asked to do little acts of kindness – rub her back, make her a cup of tea.

- may have a fragile ego – masking vulnerability by becoming cynical or sarcastic.

- tends to be rational before being emotional.

A Woman

- can be led more by her emotions than by reason.

- is usually able to articulate her inner thoughts and feelings.

- may be less inhibited than a man in showing her feelings of joy or sadness – laughing or crying.

- focuses more on her senses, reacting to how she feels inside.

- likes to have her emotional needs met before engaging in physical intimacy.

- enjoys feeling protected by her man.

- can have a strong nesting instinct – to establish a home and start a family.

- when she is upset, a woman often needs emotional comfort before engaging in a rational discussion.

- can be impatient with a man's inability or reluctance to express his feelings.

What do you think? Do any of the statements resonate with you or help you understand your partner more fully? Go through the list together. Talk about your reactions.

Often, couples think they know each other well just from being with each other, having a good time and going out together. All seems fine when there are no problems. But how do you both cope when things go wrong? What about your reactions to challenging situations?

Now is the time to find out more about each other. Maybe you could ask more questions. Then listen carefully, observing body language. How adept are you at picking up on personal cues?

PARTNERSHIP QUIZ

The questions below are designed to give you an idea of your knowledge of your partner. They may also clarify your ideas of partnership in married life.

1. How does your partner like to observe special days, such as holidays or birthdays?

2. How often does he or she like to be silly, let go and have fun?

3. Do you think you have enough fun time together?

4. What are your partner's daily habits at home – tidy, untidy: are you bothered by any of his/her daily routines?

5. Where and when does he/she prefer to eat meals – away from or surrounded by distractions?

6. What is your partner's take on timekeeping — being early, right on time or strolling in late?

7. What does he/she like to do for leisure?

8. Have you any leisure activities in common?

9. How often would you like to go out for a Date Night?

10. How do you interact with each other's families?

11. Are you happy with the role IT plays in your partner's daily life?

12. Are you happy with the role IT plays in your own life?

13. On a scale of 1 to 10, how do you rank yourself as a partner in this relationship?

14. How do you rank your fiancé(e) as a partner?

If this exercise has raised issues that bother you, it is important to discuss them. For instance, let's take Question 5. Maybe you eat meals together, but it is nearly always in front of a screen, or with one of you texting. Perhaps that's fine for your partner. However, you may consider mealtimes spent together as a wonderful opportunity to talk and connect. You would prefer to sit down across the table from your partner, away from distractions and enjoy each other's company.

This is a good conversation to have. Once you have listened attentively to what your partner feels, then you should be able to reach an agreement about mealtimes that suits you both.

EMOTIONAL CONNECTION

As couples become more of a team, they learn to create an emotional connection. This is a vital element in creating and sustaining a successful relationship. It is true that when two people are physically attracted to each other, there is a connection. But that connection is deepened through words and behaviour.

Here are some suggested ways of improving your emotional connection.

- Express your **appreciation** of something your partner has done. No matter how small or trivial it may seem to you, this is a powerful way to make your spouse feel valued and appreciated.

- Learn to handle arguments **respectfully**. Instead of raising your voice, try speaking gently. Introduce the topic softly. N.B. No yelling and no dumping – throwing in baggage from the past.

- When there are problems, be **supportive** of one another. It is good for your partner to know that he/she has in you a loyal and true friend who will always be there.

- Pick up on **cues.** For instance, if your partner is not responsive or does not seem as cheerful as normal, be sensitive when exploring what is wrong.

- Think about the **language** you use to try to understand your partner. Ask if everything is ok. Your partner may not give you much insight initially, but allow him/her time to reflect.

- Try to be **supportive**, without pushing your partner to answer your questions. Do not demand that he/she opens up immediately. You can start the dialogue. Make the connection that says – *I want you to be happy. I care about you. I want the best for you. I am here to listen to you.*

Stereotypically, men are said to be more closed off in relationships than women. However, gender-based stereotypes can be misleading. Openness depends on the individual, and anyone can shut down. It all depends on the person's background, personality, and life experiences.

Spending lots of quality **time** together helps people get to know each other. Aim for time free from distractions, time when you can listen attentively to one another. And remember, to truly get to know each other takes a lifetime. You are just at the start of this exciting journey of discovery.

If your partner finds it hard to share information, see *When Your Partner Has Difficulty Sharing* – No. 13 in the Troubleshooting Guide (p. 125).

FOCUSING ON EXPECTATIONS AND GOALS – THE TEAM PICTURE

Before the wedding is the time to sort out the important issue of what each of you expects and envisages once you are married.

1. **Children**. The question of whether, when and how many children you plan to have is an important one. To presume that your partner thinks like you do on this subject can be risky. Talk about it. Clarify. If one says he or she wants a big family, to the other person

that might mean three children. To the person who says it, it could mean five, six or even more. Discuss this so that you are on the same wavelength.

2. **Finances** are a big and sometimes tough issue. There should be no nasty surprises after the wedding. For instance, if one partner has unpaid debts, this should be disclosed as you get to know one another and before you plan your marriage. Try to answer these questions together:

- Do you plan to open a joint bank account after you are married?

- Are you happy to share your financial details with your partner?

- What do you envisage as big-ticket items in the future? How will they be paid for?

- Do you plan to buy a house? If so, how will you prepare for that?

- Do you plan to go away for holidays every year?

- Who will pay the everyday bills?

    Bear in mind that the financial decisions we make are often determined by how those decisions were made in our families of origin. If your families had different attitudes to finance, can you two agree on your approach? How adaptable and open to change are you?

3. **Where to live?** This too can be an emotive topic. Are you going to live near one set of parents? If so, are both of you happy with this arrangement? Does one of you plan to live abroad at some stage – long or

short term? Make sure that you each know the other's intentions and that you are both happy with them.

4. **Health histories.** It is important to share your family health histories, both physical and mental. This is especially true if you plan to have children.

5. **Habits and behaviours.** What is your attitude to and behaviour around the use of alcohol? What about your partner? Have you used recreational drugs in the past? Talk about this. And what is your attitude towards pornography? What about your partner? Alcohol, drugs, and pornography can all threaten the health and happiness of a couple. If any of these is an issue in your relationship, it is important that you address and resolve it before marriage.

YOUR ROLES AS PARTNERS

How do you envisage yourself as a partner in your married life?

What are your thoughts on your differing roles in certain aspects of home or financial management?

What does your fiancé(e) think?

Take the quiz below separately and then discuss your answers.

PARTNERSHIP ROLES QUIZ

- How do I envisage us as partners in our married life?

- In what ways do I see my partner contributing to managing our home?

- If I feel that I do most of the work, how could I change things without a row?

- What role did I play in my family of origin – happy child; attention seeker; carer; irresponsible child; problem solver; martyr; or was there a shared workload?

- What role do I already play in this relationship with my fiancé(e)?

- Are there times when I feel we are not on the same team?

- What would I like to see happening?

- Do I see my fiancé(e) as an equal partner in our relationship?

KEEPING YOUR OWN IDENTITY

And the two shall become one...

While the above statement can be applied to the wonderful act of sexual intimacy, it should not be interpreted as implying that once you get married you lose your own individuality and identity.

Marriage is not a matter of two people fusing into one. As Kahlil Gibran says in *The Prophet:*

...let there be spaces in your togetherness
And let the winds of the heavens dance between you.

Marriage enables two people to connect at a deep level. But that bond of love should not tie or tether one to the other. Rather, it should be like an elastic thread, allowing each to be their separate selves while being aware of the draw and attraction of the other. There is something really joyful about getting back together after being apart.

For every action there is an equal and opposite reaction. This is true for all aspects of life, including relationships. Just as you need and want to be connected to your partner, there is also a pull or desire to retain your own independence and integrity. As we seek to be connected to others, we also want and need to hold on to our own individuality, our own identity.

Since you and your fiancé(e) have been dating, is there a part of your life or an aspect of your personality that has been side-lined? Maybe you love swimming, but you have not had time to fit it in since this relationship started. What about your fiancé(e)? Has he/she sacrificed some pastime or ambition in order to focus on your relationship?

It is only to be expected that when you are getting to know one another at the start of a relationship, you are happy to dedicate most, if not all, of your free time to fostering that bond. Now that you have decided to get married and commit to spending your lives together, it is good to pause and plan. How does each of you envisage being part of a couple while keeping your own identity? Talk about it.

You will realise that your relationship is on a strong footing once you feel that you are still free to be yourself, that you are respected, loved, and trusted by your partner. Being alone allows you to keep in touch with your inner self; it gives you time to think objectively, to check up on how you feel. Then you return to your spouse re-energised, happy, and thankful.

Some couples find it a challenge to get the right balance between 'me' time and 'we' time. Recognising each other's need for separateness is part of the respect and trust that are the keystones of a healthy and happy relationship. Giving each other time out shows love and understanding.

To quote Kahlil Gibran once more:

Stand together yet not too near together…
For the oak tree and the cypress grow not in each other's shadow

What aspects of your lifestyle as a singleton do you want to keep after you get married?

Are there some things that you are not prepared to forfeit? Have you discussed these with your partner? Some couples find the checklist below helpful. See what you and your partner think – you may like to write out your own agreement.

We agree:

- to respect our differences – we know that we will not always think alike.

- to accept that we can each still go out with our friends at times.

- to accommodate each other's need to have time for ourselves, especially if we have children.

- to understand that our work commitments are important.

- to acknowledge each other's right to privacy.

- to be prepared to compromise when we have differences of opinion.

- to take turns in deciding where we should go or what we should do at weekends.

- to treat one another with respect at all times.

- to live in a way that is worthy of each other's trust.

CONCLUSION

This marks the end of *Happily Ever After*. Well done for staying the course. Has this chapter given you any food for thought? Once again, it is all about knowing and articulating your expectations and needs and listening to those of your partner.

Some discussion and forward planning now will go a long way to eliminating any bumps on the road ahead. I have every confidence that you and your partner are now well-equipped to create a wonderful future together.

The Troubleshooting Guide that follows is designed to address any issues that may benefit from further analysis.

TROUBLESHOOTING GUIDE

1. WHEN COUPLES DIFFER

- Don't take a difference of opinion personally – everyone has a right to think for themselves, even your partner. A different attitude or opinion is just that – different from yours. There is no insult to your ideas implied by difference.

- If you don't feel happy with this difference, look at your reaction. Are you upset by the fact that you disagree on an issue? Perhaps this is the first time that you have realised that you don't think alike on everything. But no couples think alike on everything – to claim that this is so could imply that one partner is so anxious to please the other that they are afraid of expressing a different opinion. If that is the case, consider the matter of control. Are you trying to control your partner in a subtle way? Or is control, or being always in the perceived right, an important issue for your partner? Talk about it.

- If you still feel upset by your differences, stop and think this through. On a scale of 1 to 10, how upset are you? Sit with your feelings for a while. Has your level of upset decreased, or is it still quite high? If it continues, you need to talk to your partner.

- Can you name the feeling or feelings underlying your upset – hurt, disappointment, outrage, sadness…?

- If you fear that discussing your different opinions may result in an argument, go to Page 19. There, you will find techniques for expressing your feelings in a nonconfrontational way. Again, bear in mind that it is essential for the health of your relationship that each of you feels free to express your own opinion, even if that is difficult for your partner to hear. Playing the *Perfect Couple* game can be dangerous.

- Perhaps you are upset because of the importance of an issue to you. Maybe this is something that you consider very significant, something on which you are not prepared to compromise. Think about this. Is the issue really important in the greater scheme of things? Talk about it.

- No matter how upset you feel, don't lose sight of the basic element of communicating effectively – using a calm tone of voice and respectful language.

2. WHO AM I?

How well do you know yourself? Have a look at the **Johari Window** below and see if it gives you any insight.

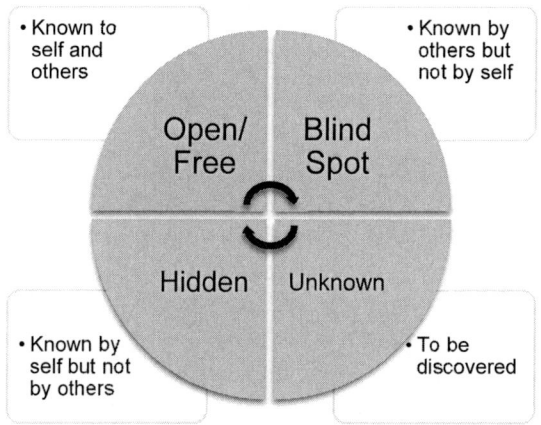

The concept of dividing the Ego into four sections was created by psychologists Joseph Luft (1916–2014) and Harrington Ingham (1916–1995) in 1955. This simple illustration is designed to help people better understand their relationships with themselves and others.

Open/Free Self

This is the part of you with which you are most comfortable and at ease. Therefore, you are happy to share this aspect of yourself with others. This public persona is open and accessible to all who meet you.

Blind Spot

We all have our blind spots, that part of self that is obvious to others but of which we are unaware. It is only when others point out your blind spots that you become aware of them. It may be that you come across as aggressive or bossy when you think you are simply being moderately assertive. Accepting such feedback is never easy. But when it comes from a trusted friend, you owe it to yourself to take note. It is good to have someone reflect back to you; to help you get to know yourself more fully; to become more conscious of how your behaviour can affect others.

Hidden Self

You are aware of this secret part of the self, this inner place where you can be most truly yourself. But you tend to keep this aspect hidden from public view. That is good – after all, you are not going to share personal details with everyone you meet. In fact, you may put on a façade to prevent others from prying or getting too close to your more intimate side. But now that you have found a life partner, you will hopefully feel comfortable to share your inner thoughts and secrets, knowing that they will be treated with respect and confidentiality.

Unknown Self

This last aspect of the self is exactly that – unknown, both to yourself and to others. It relates to your hidden strength and depth. This aspect of self is often revealed or realised when you least expect it, as when faced with a challenge or at a critical time in your life. The unknown self is often realised in retrospect. Once an immediate crisis has passed, you can be pleasantly surprised at how you dealt with it. Maybe it has shown what a competent and decisive person you are.

REFLECTION

What are your thoughts on the Johari Window? Can you identify with these four aspects of the self? Life is a journey of discovery, starting with discovering your true self. It can take a whole lifetime to really know the complete you, but the more insight you have, the greater your chance of happiness. Once you know and feel happy to accept who you are, you are able to connect more effectively with others.

Think about sharing your hidden or private self; more fully with your partner; try to be open to accept the messages you receive about your blind spots; and be prepared to discover your as yet unknown inner strengths – you are probably much more resilient than you ever realised.

3. FEELING OVERWHELMED – USING THE TRIAGE METHOD

It is a well-recognised fact that one of the most important roles in Accident and Emergency Departments of hospitals, is that of the triage nurse. This is the person who examines the patient on arrival. This is the person who assigns the patient to one of three categories:

1. absolute emergency
2. urgent but not acute
3. non-urgent

Think of the qualities necessary to triage effectively – staying calm in tense situations; thinking rationally despite the emotions of the moment; speaking with concern but with warm authority.

It is really effective to apply this same triage technique to the perceived emergencies in our lives? Of course, the big difference here is that you may feel more like the patient than the triage nurse. But the more you rise to the challenge of distinguishing between what is important and what is not, the happier you will be.

Here are the three steps of the Triage Method:

1. If you feel very stressed or upset, stay with that feeling without speaking until you have calmed your inner emotions.
2. Next, consider the situation as rationally as you can. What is the real issue here? Is this a true emergency, worthy of all my stress and anxiety? Or is this something that can wait until I find a better time to talk about it?
3. Now, and only now that you have triaged, address the situation with your partner. Watch the tone of your voice – a high-pitched tone suggests that you are still very emotional. Try planning what you will say, naming your feelings but without sounding like the victim in this situation.

Using the triage method can help avoid unnecessary rows and drama in your relationship. Try it and you'll see.

4. FEELING UNEXPECTEDLY UPSET

If you have felt upset at times recently, if there are issues that have unexpectedly caused you unhappiness, there is no need for panic. Be curious about what is going on for you. Stay with your feelings. First of all, accept the fact that our feelings fluctuate – it is part of the human condition. Even though you are about to marry the most wonderful person in the world for you, remember that no one is expected to be totally happy all the time. Now ask yourself the questions below:

- Can I name my deepest feeling right now – Am I upset because of resentment, hurt, jealousy…?
- Now that I have identified my underlying feeling, do I understand myself a bit better?

- What would I like to see happening around this issue?

- Have I communicated my thoughts and feelings to anyone else?

- Can I look at this from another perspective?

- Is there a lighter side to this issue?

- Are there steps that I could take to help resolve this issue? Talking, listening, changing my attitude?

- Am I feeling less bothered by this matter now that I have explored it more fully?

5. WHEN TRUST ISSUES ARISE

- The first thing to do, as always, is to **communicate** effectively. Stay calm. Tell your partner that you would like to hear more about the issue or event that is causing you concern. It is only natural that you are each curious to know as much about the other as possible. After all, you are planning to spend the rest of your lives together. As Peter Saarstadt famously sang:

  Tell me the thoughts that surround you.
  I want to look inside your head

- The **tone** of voice you use when addressing a sensitive issue is of vital importance. Avoid sounding accusatory. Remember, everyone is innocent until proven otherwise. You do not know your partner's story yet.

- Once you have agreed to address an important issue, the most effective strategy in my experience is to make the issue the subject of a **Listening Exercise** – *See Chapter Five.*

- Are you still not satisfied, still not convinced that you can fully trust your partner? If so, here are two possible reasons:

    o Either, your partner has a different view of what honesty and loyalty are. Perhaps your partner considers it ok to flirt with a work colleague, or to discuss intimate details of your relationship with friends. Whatever the issue, you need to establish what is acceptable and unacceptable to both of you.

- Or, you have trust issues. In other words, you find it difficult to trust others because of some breach of trust in your past. Does that resonate with you? If so, think back as far as you can to an incident in your childhood or adolescence when you felt betrayed by someone you trusted. Discuss this with your partner – it will help both of you to understand better what is going on.

6. DIFFICULTY RECOGNISING FEELINGS

If you have difficulty recognising any feelings associated with your chosen incident from your childhood, please try again. Either the event did not have a significant impact on you in the first place, or you have not given yourself enough time to really focus on it and relive it.

Try to recall more detail. Can you describe the setting? Who were the main players?

If you feel like it, try drawing a picture of the incident. Drawing can often help you see a situation more clearly. Use coloured crayons if you have them. Don't worry about your artistic talent – just draw stick figures if you like. This is not an art contest.

Now look at your picture and answer the following questions:

1. What does it tell you?

2. Where are you in the picture – in the centre or on the periphery?

3. How big are you compared to the others in the picture?

4. What colours have you chosen to use for yourself – light or dark?

5. Now fill in some speech bubbles. Who said what?'

6. How did you react at the time?

7. How did the others involved react?

8. How do you feel about your reaction?

9. Is there anything about the incident which makes you feel uncomfortable? If so, can you put a more precise feeling word on the discomfort – regret, shame, anger, self-pity, sadness, loneliness?

10. Put yourself back there once more. What might have helped you deal with those feelings?

11. Was there anyone in whom you could confide?

12. What might you have said to a trusted person?

13. What might you have done then that you did not do?

Try to work on becoming more aware of what you are feeling. Remember, it is ok to experience emotions and it is ok to acknowledge your feelings even if they are not happy ones.

7. DEALING WITH A NIGGLING SENSE OF UNHAPPINESS

There is so much going on in your life right now that you may run the risk of ignoring your own inner needs. Of course, you have your fiancé(e) who loves you and in whom you can confide, yet you may experience a niggling sense of unhappiness within yourself. If this occurs, address it. Ask the question:

What do I need to change in order to feel happier with myself?

Note that this question is addressed to yourself. So be sure that the answer focuses on actions or attitudes that *you* can change. Avoid transferring responsibility for your happiness onto someone else. For example, say:

If I can think more positively about myself, I will feel happier.
NOT

If my partner told me I was great, I would feel happier.

Of course, we all like to receive positive feedback from others. And we like it especially when it comes from our partner. But this is a chicken and egg situation. If you allow yourself to feel more confident, if you start liking yourself more, you will automatically emit more positive energy to those around you. You will then elicit the response that you desire. Your partner will be inclined to say:

- *I love it when you smile.*

- *It's so good to come back to a happy home.*

- *You look great today – it makes me feel happy too.*

This is the great truth about love – that it starts with loving and accepting the self, then it grows on the basis of giving to others. You radiate positivity when you are happy with yourself. And in order to radiate happiness, you must first be open to others. The negative unhappy self is a closed entity. The accepting, happy self is open.

A man was walking along a country road one sunny day. All was fine until a dog on the road ahead started barking at him. Not being a great dog lover, the man immediately felt threatened. He picked up a stone and held it in his clenched fist. However, as he came nearer to the dog, he changed his mind about him.

This dog is barking, but he is also wagging his tail, he thought. *Maybe if I drop the stone and open my hand, he will feel less threatened by me.*

So, he dropped the stone and spoke calmly to the dog, who had now stopped barking and approached to be patted on the head.

REFLECTION

Try to become conscious of the closed fist attitude. There is often no need to anticipate trouble or negativity. Approaching others with an open hand and mind, free of prejudice and self-protective devices, will yield much greater rewards than clinging to the closed and guarded self.

Love grows on the basis of giving. To receive love, we must be able to give love. For it is in giving that we receive most of all.

Obstacles to love are created by ourselves. A fear of rejection stems from our memory.

- *Can I look beyond negative experiences of the past and allow myself to be truly open to love again?*

- *Am I afraid of being vulnerable in case I get hurt again?*

- *If I can trust my partner enough to be open and honest about my feelings and my fears, then our love can grow and thrive.*

8. CONSTANT CONFLICT

If confrontation occurs too frequently it can cause problems in your relationship. Try following the guidelines below:

- Avoid becoming too emotional and upset when you have a disagreement.

- Put the disagreement into perspective. How important is this issue?

- Start from the beginning. Address the issue again – this time making it the subject of a Listening Exercise – *See Chapter Four*

- Now that you have heard your partner's thoughts, can your outlook change?
- Reassess the situation – has the difference between you grown or diminished?

- Assess your motive here – are you defending a basic principle or are you just determined to win at any cost?

- Is it possible to reach a compromise?

- Can you agree to disagree on this issue?

9. WHEN WE STILL DISAGREE – WHAT NEXT?

So, here you are, having both listened to one another, but you feel stuck. You realise that no matter how hard you try; you cannot convince your partner to agree with you on a certain issue. Of course, it may also be that you refuse to be convinced by your partner's argument or ideas.

What happens next? Here are some tips that should help:

- **Scale it** – if you were to rank this issue on a scale of 1 – (unimportant) to 10 – (very important), where would it be?

- **Examine negative attitudes** – ask yourself, *why am I so opposed to this idea? Is my attitude rational, emotional, or inherited?* Here are some examples:

    - **Rational** – I object to my partner spending so much time in front of a screen because I think that it has a very negative impact on our marriage. Not only does it make him/her more distant, it spoils the happy atmosphere in our home and damages our relationship. I think we should put away our screens and talk to one another more.

    - **Emotional** – I cannot stand it when my partner watches football. It is true it does not take up the whole weekend, but just seeing him slumped in front of the TV makes me feel depressed.

    - **Inherited** – when I was growing up, nearly all the rows in our house centred around television. Everyone wanted to watch a different programme, people were often grumpy, we didn't communicate well as a family. Now we all have our own screens, and viewing time is limited. But my attitude has not changed.

- **Share it** – talk to your partner about your reasons for disagreeing. Try tracing the source of your negative attitude. Is it based on your own reasoning? Is it perhaps overly emotional? Or is it based on attitudes you have assumed from your parents, without questioning or evaluating for yourself? This analysis can help you assess your outlook more objectively.

- **Listen with care** – Ask your partner to explain once again the reasoning behind his/her viewpoint. Can you identify somewhat with what you hear?

- **Scale it again** – now that you have looked at your reaction and reconsidered your partner's viewpoint, has the issue diminished in importance on the 1 to 10 scale?

- **Can we reach a compromise?** To what extent are you prepared to accept your partner's attitude without major objections? Is your partner willing to yield somewhat too?

- **Any hint of a stubborn streak?** Stay aware of your motives in this disagreement. Is this issue truly worth disagreeing over, or are you sticking to your guns because of some unspoken anger or resentment towards your partner? Be honest with yourself.

- **If there is underlying tension**, try to separate it from the present issue. At a later time, address the incident from the past that has caused the underlying anger or resentment.

10. DEALING WITH RESIDUAL FEARS

Are there times when you become anxious at the thought of sharing your life so intimately with another person? Do certain aspects of being married make you feel uneasy?

We are by nature social creatures, so we seek a connection with others. But as a long-term relationship develops, some of us back away from the increasing intimacy and sharing that this entails.

How about you? Perhaps you are happy to become intimate physically, but not emotionally. Or perhaps the idea of sexual intimacy is quite frightening.

Once you feel fear around an issue, you may go to great lengths to protect yourself from being exposed. Perhaps you tend to go into self-protection mode – hiding behind a facade of distraction, self-effacement or lies. In this case, by definition, you will be less open with your partner.

Do you have some **fears** regarding this relationship? Write down your own list and then check below.

I am afraid that:

- if my partner knew what I am really like, it would be the end of our relationship.

- my partner will find out that I feel very sad/lonely at times.

- one day I will get so angry, like I used to, that it will finish our relationship.

- my partner will find me too controlling in our relationship.

- my partner will discover that I find it difficult to believe his/her words of love.

- my partner will learn about the shame I feel about something in my past that I don't want to talk about.

- if I relax during sexual intercourse, I will lose control.

- my partner will not find me physically exciting once he/she gets used to having sex with me.

Once you have listed any fears, set about sharing them with your partner. This may require some courage. You need to feel that your love is strong. You need to know that you will respect each other's feelings. *See Sharing can be Scary, in Chapter Three.*

11. WHEN A SECRET IS TOO BIG

There are some secrets that are difficult to disclose. If you had a traumatic experience in your past, you may need professional help. This is important. You should not carry untreated trauma alone. Untreated trauma will fester. It will not go away of its own accord.

No amount of glossing over the surface will free you from its inhibiting effects.

N.B. Please seek professional help if you feel that you cannot share your secret with your partner. Talking about it will help you put it into perspective. Withholding something secret and keeping it inside yourself means that you cannot be truly open to expressing or receiving love and enjoying a deep connection with another.

If your secret involves an offence or crime committed against you, such as psychological, physical, or sexual abuse, you should seek professional help and support. And remember, that by reporting such abuse you can help prevent others from suffering a similar fate.

12. WHAT MAKES INTIMACY SO SPECIAL

- It is a unique element in the couple relationship. Otherwise, we might as well be friends or roommates.

- This beautiful act of love is all about being caring, gentle and loving towards each other.

- In this most intimate, bonding experience we are joined together in an emotional connection.

- Sexual intimacy allows us to be vulnerable together, sharing our bare selves with one another.

- It unites the couple at a deeper level, fulfilling our primal instinct for connection.

- It makes us feel safe, secure, valued in a soothing, safe attachment.

- Sexual intimacy helps us to de-stress and reconnect. The couple can relax knowing that *You are there for me and I am there for you.*

- Finally, it is about having fun together, exploring, experimenting, enjoying each other's bodies. Each couple travels their own unique ongoing sexual journey, adapting to changing circumstances, while always discovering more about each other.

13. WHEN YOUR PARTNER HAS DIFFICULTY SHARING

If your partner finds it difficult to be completely open with you, you can help by taking the following steps:

<u>Listen and give feedback</u>

- Ask your partner – *Please tell me what you are feeling, not what you are thinking.*

- Listen as feelings are expressed.

- Give feedback: – *What I have heard you say is that you feel angry, hurt…when…*

- Clarification: Ask your partner to correct anything you have omitted.

<u>Visualisation</u> – if your partner is still unwilling to talk.

- Ask your partner, *what is the worst thing that could happen if you share this secret with me?*

- Explore the fears around this.

- *If you tell me, do you think you would feel worse than you do now?*

- *How would you like things to be between us?*

- *How can we help make this happen?*
- *How would that make you feel?*

Look to the future with confidence

- How does each of you see your relationship in five years' time?

- Reassure your partner that she/he is valued and loved.

- Explore self-belief – *How do you feel about yourself? What are your best qualities?*

- Ask – *Which of your achievements are you most proud of?*

- Encourage – *I think that we can do this together. How about you?*

14. COMMON PITFALLS

THE FOUR HORSEMEN OF THE APOCALYPSE – John Gottman

When it comes to advice for keeping a relationship happy and thriving, it is difficult to improve on the classic four greatest threats to a healthy relationship, as outlined by the famous American psychotherapist John Gottman. They are named after the four horsemen who signified the apocalypse, or end of the world. Once you are aware of them, you are less likely to allow them become part of the dynamic of your relationship.

If you ever feel tempted to resort to Criticism, Defensiveness, Stonewalling or Contempt, consider opting instead for the Antidote.

1. **Criticism** – when others upset us, or when we just don't understand them, it can be tempting to resort to criticism. This can include labelling or insulting the

other person. *You're so selfish...* or, *you think you're so great.*

Antidote – if you feel upset with your partner, communicate your feelings as a complaint, rather than as a criticism – *When you behave like that, I feel hurt, resentful...*

2. **Defensiveness** – None of us likes to receive negative feedback. When confronted with a negative message, the temptation is to resort to the default position of defensiveness, *you talk about me? How about you? You...*

   Antidote – If we respect their opinion, it is important to be able to accept some negative reflections, especially from our partner. Careful and attentive listening is required here. Remember the Blind Spot pane in the Johari Window? Reflect on the message instead of becoming defensive.

3. **Stonewalling** – This behaviour is really destructive to a healthy relationship. Not responding to the other person, switching off, making no eye contact, all send a clear message – *I don't care what you say; I am not interested in how you feel; in fact, you are not worth listening to.*

   Antidote – Resolve never to give your partner the silent treatment. No matter how upset you are, avoid using silence as a weapon.

4. **Contempt** – Treating others with contempt indicates both that you consider them to be worthless and that you look on yourself as somehow superior. Showing contempt usually involves the use of cynicism or biting sarcasm. While this is belittling for your

partner, it also diminishes you as a person. It does not show how witty and clever you are.

Antidote – Be aware of the corrosive effect of contempt on a relationship. Such behaviour is not worthy of a loving couple, especially people as loving as both of you.

REFLECTION

If you or your partner tend to resort to any of the above tactics, see if you can develop a system whereby you give a signal to the other once you become aware of it. This can be a subtle cough, a hand signal or simply a reminder:

Let's not go down this road again. Remember what we decided?

This way, you can avoid heading down the path of negative behaviour. It buys time to reflect, re-assess and be constructive instead.

Afterword

Marriage is a coming of age, a challenge, and a commitment. It is a celebration of love and a statement of intent to share your lives with one another. I hope that this book has given you some insights along with some tangible tools to help enrich your relationship.

May you both live happily ever after.

Bibliography

Berne, D., 2016. *Transactional Analysis in Psychotherapy.* San Francisco: Hauraki Publishing

Bowlby, John (1988) *A Secure Base: Parent-Child Attachment and Healthy Human Development,* London: Routledge; New York, NY: Basic Books

British Association of Anger Management (BAAM) (2008) *Mental Health Organisation: Boiling Point Report 2008* last accessed 26th Jan 2021

Byers and Demmons, 1999; Carrere & Gottman, 1999; Christensin & Shenk, 1991 *Communication – cause of 90% relationship problems*

Chopra, Deepak (2014) *The Secret of Attraction: Meditation* video YouTube last accessed Jan 25th 2021

Eisenberger, Naomi I. *Future Science: Essays From The Cutting Edge*, Edited by Max Brockman (Vintage Books, 2011)

Frankl Victor 2004: *Man's Search for Meaning;* Rider

Gibran, Kahlil The Prophet 1994: Mandarin Paperback

Gottman, John M; Silver, Nan (1999) *The Seven Principles for Making Marriage Work,* New York, NY: Three Rivers Press

Green, B., 2010. *Anger: recognition, treatment and management*. British Journal of Wellbeing, 1(7), pp.39-43

Harris, T., n.d. *I'm OK – You're OK*

Holmes, D. and Edmondson, A., 2000. *The Johari Window.* (Cincinnati, Ohio).

Horton, Paul B, Hunt, Chester L; *Sociology* – 6th Edition Publ. McGraw Hill Education 2004 marriage definition
Johnson, Susan, 2008, *Hold Me Tight,* Little, Brown and Co., New York 10017

Marriage Advice - Expert Marriage Tips & Advice. 2020. *20 Most Common Marriage Problems Faced by Married Couples.* [online] Available at: <https://marriage.com/advice/relationship/8-common-problems-in-married-life
Merriam-Webster Dictionary definition of *Engaged*

Moberg, Kerstin Uvnas. *The Oxytocin Factor: Tapping the Hormone of Calm, Love, and Healing* (Da Capo Press 2003)

Pascale, Rob; Primavera, Lou, PhD *So Happy Together* https://www.psychologytoday.com › intl › blog

Thich Nhãt Hanh (2017) *The Art of Living,* London: Rider Books

Wilcox, W.Bradford; Dew, Jeffrey; ElHage, Alysse *Cohabitation Doesn't Compare,* Institute for Family Studies, Feb 2019

Wood, Dustin; Harms, Peter; Vazire, Simine (2010) *Perceiver Effects as Projective Tests: What Your Perceptions of Others Say about You,* Journal of Personality and Social Psychology, Vol 99, No. 1, pp.174-190.